JUMPIN JEHOVAH

EXPOSING THE ATROCITIES OF THE OLD TESTAMENT GOD

BY

PAUL TICE

The Book Tree
San Diego, CA

JUMPIN' JEHOVAH:
EXPOSING THE ATROCITIES
OF THE OLD TESTAMENT GOD

ISBN 978-1-58509-112-6

Third Edition
Revised & Updated

Cover layout & design by Toni Villalas

Published by

The Book Tree
Post Office Box 16476
San Diego, CA 92176

We provide fascinating and educational products to help awaken the public to new ideas and information that would not be available otherwise. We carry over 1000 Books, Booklets, Audio, Video, and other products on Alchemy, Alternative Medicine, Ancient America, Ancient Astronauts, Ancient Civilizations, Ancient Mysteries, Ancient Religion and Worship, Angels, Anthropology, Anti-Gravity, Archaeology, Area 51, Assyria, Astrology, Atlantis, Babylonia, Townsend Brown, Christianity, Cold Fusion, Colloidal Silver, Comparative Religions, Crop Circles, The Dead Sea Scrolls, Early History, Electromagnetics, Electro-Gravity, Egypt, Electromagnetic Smog, Michael Faraday, Fatima, The Fed, Fluoride, Free Energy, Freemasonry, Global Manipulation, The Gnostics, God, Gravity, The Great Pyramid, Gyroscopic Anti-Gravity, Healing Electromagnetics, Health Issues, Hinduism, HIV, Human Origins, Jehovah, Jesus, Jordan Maxwell, John Keely, Lemuria, Lost Cities, Lost Continents, Magick, Masonry, Mercury Poisoning, Metaphysics, Mythology, Occultism, Paganism, Pesticide Pollution, Personal Growth, The Philadelphia Experiement, Philosophy, Powerlines, Prophecy, Psychic Research, Pyramids, Rare Books, Religion, Religious Controversy, Roswell, Walter Russell, Scalar Waves, SDI, John Searle, Secret Societies, Sex Worship, Sitchin Studies, Smart Cards, Joseph Smith, Solar Power, Sovereignty, Space Travel, Spirituality, Stonehenge, Sumeria, Sun Myths, Symbolism, Tachyon Fields, Templars, Tesla, Theology, Time Travel, The Treasury, UFOs, Underground Bases, World Control, The World Grid, Zero Point Energy, and much more. Call 1 (800) 700-TREE for our *FREE BOOK TREE CATALOG* or visit our website at www.thebooktree.com for more information.

CONTENTS

Introduction 5

Chapter One 7
    Who Was Jehovah?

Chapter Two 19
    Total Control

Chapter Three 35
    God or Demon?

Chapter Four 51
    The Serpent, Jehovah, and Satan

Chapter Five 57
    Let's Fire God

Chapter Six 63
    Perfect God, or Perfect Loser?

Chapter Seven 81
    How to Expose a False God

Appendix 93
    Biblical References to Jehovah

Bibliography 98

Index 99

Also by Paul Tice

Shadow of Darkness, Dawning of Light: The Awakening of Human Consciousness in the 21st Century and Beyond, ISBN 978-1-885395-88-7, 2007, The Book Tree.

Triumph of the Human Spirit: The Greatest Acheivements of the Human Soul and How Its Power can Change Your Life, ISBN 978-1-885395-57-3, 1999, The Book Tree.

That Old-Time Religion: The Story of Religious Foundations, with Jordan Maxwell and Dr. Alan Albert Snow; ISBN 978-1-58509-100-3, 2000, The Book Tree.

Mysteries Explored: The Search for Human Origins, UFOs, and Religious Beginnings, with Jack Barranger, ISBN 978-1-58509-101-0, 2000, The Book Tree.

Early Buddhism, with T.W. Rhys Davids (1886 reprint), smaller section titled Buddhist Ethics: The Way to Salvation?, ISBN 978-1-58509-076-1, 2000, The Book Tree.

Hus the Heretic, with Poggius the Papist (1930 reprint), section on John Hus, taken from *Triumph of the Human Spirit*, ISBN 978-1-58509-232-1, 2003, The Book Tree.

History of the Waldenses:From the Earliest Period to the Present Time, with the Author of *The Lives of Wickliffe, Hus, Jerome, etc.*(1829 reprint), section on Waldenses taken from *Triumph of the Human Spirit*, ISBN 978-1-58509-099-0, 2003, The Book Tree.

The Vital Force: Its History and Evidence, article, Paranoia Magazine: The Conspiracy Reader, Issue 36, Fall, 2004.

The Bogomils: Gnostics of Old Bulgaria, article, Gnosis Magazine, Issue 31, Spring 1994.

DEDICATION

To those who have always suspected that a God of love—the true God—could not possibly have been the cruel, jealous, violent, vindictive, and vengeful god of the Old Testament.

INTRODUCTION

In our religion everything is prosaic, and very, very serious. You can't fool around with Yahweh.

—Joseph Campbell

This work is an examination of the Old Testament god, Jehovah, and is intended to show him as he really was. It seems the term "God-fearing people" likely originated after people had encountered this Jehovah character (also known as Yahweh). After we create a clear picture of Jehovah, it will be no wonder to you, the reader, that people feared God. Yet, if God is all loving and all forgiving, why should we, or anyone else, have to fear Him? Was Jehovah really God?

If there is a real, all-loving God, it certainly was not Jehovah (or Yahweh). The atrocities he committed are inexcusable acts of cruelty and have no place in the paradigm of an all-loving God.

No doubt, Jehovah had superhuman powers; he was an entity who was far beyond being mere human, based on the Biblical accounts. But that does not mean he was God. He clearly tried to pass himself off as God to us humans—and may have even believed it himself! But he was *not* God, and the following pages will illustrate that clearly.

I am sorry if this idea upsets you or goes against your beliefs. But let us look at the *facts* before we plug in "belief." I sincerely do hope that these facts totally shatter your religious outlook concerning Jehovah. This should happen with virtually any discerning reader because any person or entity who would commit such acts in our modern world, as Jehovah had done in the past, would certainly be in prison for it or, more likely, executed.

Jehovah was not a pleasant creature. He did not spread joy and happiness wherever he went. He spread fear, death and slavery, just to name a few.

Let's take a look at the career of Yahweh/Jehovah with one thing in mind: If a family member of yours were to act this way, would you treat him like a god? Or would you try to get him professional help?

One thing must be made clear before we start. This work is in no way meant to be anti-Semitic. I have nothing against the Jewish people. They are, like everyone else, fine and good by me. It's their god I have a problem with. The evidence shows that he was a fraud, an imposter and even acted at times in a mentally deranged fashion. These blistering accusations against this entity serve no purpose without facts. Let us move on to the facts, so you may judge them for yourself.

INTRODUCTION TO THIRD EDITION

Ten years have passed since the first edition of this book appeared, originally in booklet form. It was expected to remain as a fun little booklet, but due to demand it was expanded into a book, with the second edition in 2000. Phase three has now come to pass.

The research and evidence provided leave little room for debate, although there are those who would debate me anyway. My supporters, rather than critics, have suggested that I dispense with the more inane comedic sections and focus primarily on the valid research. This has been done, for the most part, despite the continued need to break up the seriousness with some off-the-wall sarcasm or humor. Those die-hard scholarly types wishing for a completely serious version of this book will just have to grin and bear it.

The original cover was done by a comic book artist, showing Jehovah jumping up and down on a pogo stick, with the sun looking down on him in utter shock and surprise. That is gone. The artist's mother, who accused me of poisoning her son's mind by even suggesting such a piece, can now rest knowing that her son's work has been, at least in this instance, stifled. Now being used is the more serious and rather beautiful depiction of Abraham getting ready to kill his son Isaac just because Jehovah said so. Not quite as funny. But it supports the material, including the book's view of it, which begins on page 81.

Additional research has been added in place of jokes, since the new findings were too important to omit. Yet new humor, in some cases, proved too much of a temptation. It strikes me as being so absurd—that people could seriously, in this day and age, still consider Jehovah to be God—that I have no choice but to be even more absurd in the writing of some sections of this book. Certain scholars are groaning right now, knowing that some great laughs still remain. Lighten up! With all the fear and carnage unleashed in the world by Jehovah, it is now time to balance the scales with a few chuckles and spontaneous screeches while, at the same time, exposing the atrocities of this so-called diety.

Jehovah failed to prove himself as a God of love, as evidenced in these pages. However, it is this author's belief—or better yet, he knows—that such a loving God does indeed exist. It is time to put the fables and legends to rest, and seek out what what we can truly grasp within our own hearts.

Paul Tice

August, 2007

ONE

WHO WAS JEHOVAH?

The Jehovah of the Jews is a suspi - cious tyrant, who breathes nothing but blood, murder, and carnage, and who demands that they should nour - ish him with the vapours of animals.

—Paul Henri Thiry,
Baron D'Holback

We are all children in a vast kinder - garten trying to spell God's name with the wrong alphabet blocks.

—Tennessee Williams

YHWH are the four consonants which compose the Hebrew name for God. YHWH was considered as being too sacred to pro- nounce, but after a time everyone started doing it anyway—adding a couple of vowels, making it "Yahweh." The English rendering of those four consonants is "Jehovah," and that is how we shall address him in this work.

Jehovah started off as a tribal god or leader of a small group of semi-nomads located south of Palestine, in the lands of Negeb. The early time for him was during the second millennium BC. Whoever or whatever he was on the grand scale of things, at this particular time, was of no real significance. He was a cosmic nobody, an insignificant godly vagabond waiting to be "discov- ered." All of the roaming tribes at that time had their divine pro- tectors; Jehovah was just one of many and there was absolutely nothing about him that distinguished him from any other local deity.

Yet it was clear that he was deity. Something set him apart from the tribal members—a group of people who clearly worshipped him as a god. He also referred to *himself* as a god.

. . . I am the Lord thy God,

which have brought thee out

of the land of Egypt,. . .

Exodus 20:2

Was he human? No. If the reported feats and powers we read of in the Bible are true, there is no way he could have been a nor-

Jehovah: Who was he really?

mal human being. We will go on the premise that he was not a normal human. What was he then?

Some will say that Jehovah was not an individual, per se, but a reflection of the moors and customs of the Israelites at the time. That is sheer bunk. Read the Bible. It continually refers to Jehovah as being a *specific* entity or individual. One might argue that Jehovah, or the customs of the day, were "speaking through" certain individuals—yet when this occurs in specific instances (like with Moses) it states clearly that Moses is acting as an intermediary. But in most cases a *clear distinction* is made that Moses and Jehovah are two separate and completely different individuals. If anyone thinks otherwise (after reading the Bible), they should be considered sorely lacking in analytical skills and should return to the scriptures and make a closer study. I've debated some of these people on the internet, only to discover that one would have better luck squeezing grape juice out of rocks.

Jehovah was not a "myth." He was an actual being and there's no way around this. His anatomy is discussed in the Bible. He is said to have arms (Psalms 89:13), a bosom (Psalms 74:11), eyes (2 Chr. 16:9), a face (Exodus 33:20), ears (I Pet. 3:12), feet (Psalms 18:9), hair (Dan. 7:9), a finger (Exodus 31:18), back parts (Exodus 33:23), bowels (Jer. 31:20), a head (Dan 7:9), shoulders (Deut. 33:12), lips (Isaiah 30:27), a mouth (Mat. 4:4), nostrils (2 Sam.

22:9), and a tongue (Isaiah 30:27). These are body parts, not "social customs."

For those who are still not convinced, get out your Bible and actually look these up. The controversy will end right here. What follows are accounts in the Bible about appearances made by Jehovah in obvious physical form.

Genesis 11:5, 17:1, 17:22, 18:1, 18:21-23, 26:2, 26:24, 35:7-14. In Exodus 19:11 he was "in sight of all the people," in Exodus 24:9-11 seventy-four people saw God, and in Exodus 33:9-11 he was seen "face to face."

Jehovah also performed many different things as a physical individual. For those accounts (as supporting evidence), please turn to the Appendix—which also includes many others references on his atrocities, physical attributes, and downright evil nature.

The point is that if Jehovah was not a normal human (based on the powers that he exhibited), and not a reflection of the culture, then he had to have been a "god", as the ancients called them, part of a powerful group of human-looking entities that had somehow found their way to earth in earlier times. Mythology from around the world, from all parts of the globe, tells about the gods who were here on Earth. Were these stories just a strange coincidence between cultures—even when some early cultures were so primitive and isolated that it would have been impossible to transmit and share *exact* stories? That is exactly what occurred in many cases, as with the flood and creation stories.

With the coming of the gods came great knowledge and cultural advances, as well as negative things like sophisticated techniques for war, human sacrifice, and everyone's favorite, lawyers.

Because we will accept Jehovah as a god, however, does not mean that he was *The* God. He claimed to be *the* creator God of this world in numerous Biblical passages. He did this for either one of two reasons:

1) He was so possessive of his people and jealous of other gods that he tried to ram this idea down the throats of his people so they wouldn't run off and abandon him, or

2) He was so deranged and deluded that he, himself, actually believed it.

Palestine itself knew many gods before Jehovah, but Jehovah just happened to wander through at an opportune time. He made no extravagant claims in these early years, as far as we know, but later wandered north and things fell together even more so when he gained additional followers. As his followers grew, so did his ego and lust for power. All of the gods worked in this way—taking followers and certain territory, then fighting each other for it.

Over 50 names of gods have been recovered from the Palestine area from the second millennium BC. The most powerful and popular gods during Jehovah's years were El, Baal, and Mot, to name a few. There were also a number of goddesses running around that were far more popular than Jehovah, including Astarte, Ashera (Baal's wife) and Anath.

So how did Jehovah make this leap from relative obscurity into the fast lane of godly super-stardom? What made the guy so special all of a sudden, when a short time ago he was just another slob, begging for worshippers and hoping to be recognized by someone—like people on all these cheap reality talent shows? What talents *did* Jehovah have? Well, he could fly, for one. A rather impressive feat, since we humans didn't figure that one out for another 4000 years.

Jehovah could also kill people almost as easily as looking at them, and made it a point to keep in practice. This convinced his followers to be very devout and faithful.

He had many other powers which we will detail later—let it suffice that all of his powers created awe, respect, and above all, fear, in his people.

Jehovah's People

Who exactly were his people? This is the next important question. As stated earlier, they were small groups of nomadic wanderers in the areas south of Palestine. These people had been in the Palestine area long before Jehovah showed up, and made their living as farmers and cattle raisers. These early Israelites worshipped many gods simultaneously, including Baal, who specialized in providing fertility to their fields and herds.

The northern tribes, however, were the ones that Jehovah would eventually rule over. Wandering holy men came up from the south with great tales of the mighty Jehovah. These northern Israelites did not rush down there to see this great deity, because it took another two centuries before Jehovah would claim them as his own. They were perfectly content staying in the general area where they were, farming and tending their cattle.

Later on, one of the northern tribes—the tribe of Judah—was the first to be sucked into an alliance with Jehovah, mainly because they were widely known for their aggressiveness and warlike nature. They journeyed south and united all of the southern tribes under their leadership—the Simeonites, Kenites, Jeremeelites, and

Cabelites. As these tribes were brought together, the power and importance of Jehovah increased.

Right around this time, a curious fellow named Moses is forced to flee from Egypt, leaving behind fellow Levite tribesmen in bondage. He finds refuge with one of these southern groups—the Kenites. It is here where he experiences some kind of vision, telling him that Jehovah is the one that can deliver his people, the Levites, out of bondage.

In order to understand the situation, we need to take a closer look at Moses. This guy was no fool. He was very discouraged before having this "vision." Here he is, with no help anywhere; one man against the world. Desperate for help, he shows up in the midst of this large tribal alliance, led by a powerful new god, that gathers around and listens to his story. Now you tell me if Moses was just going to sit around eating matza balls, staring a gift horse in the mouth, or actually *do* something about the situation. So Moses had a "vision"—Jehovah is meant to save his people.

That's all you had to tell this very warlike tribe of Judah who, along with Jehovah, were just itching for a fight to prove themselves and flex their newly discovered muscles. They rushed in and freed the Levites, who also became devoted followers.

How to Become a Successful God in 30 Days or Less

By this time, Jehovah had begun to blossom into a god of power and war. He was actually a storm god. Storm gods are generally worshipped as bringers of rain, helping the farmers, etc.. This was exactly how Jehovah began, but this milder aspect was lost in all of the lightning, power, and thunder that he liked to show off with. Jehovah got carried away and, as we will soon see, latched onto a big power trip. Heck, it was the best way to get glorified, revered, and worshipped. Forget about making it rain and growing a few crops. If you want some attention, go out and kick some ass.

Later, after finishing with Egypt, they traveled north. This federation of Judean tribes, led by Jehovah, took the lands located between the southern Negeb area and the area held by the tribes of Israel. This was a lot of land and, although there were religious and cultural differences between them, these new people joined the alliance for two reasons: 1) Security—much like a shop owner who must pay off the mob to stay physically and financially healthy and 2) Greed. They wanted to get in on this movement. All parties involved had their hearts set on additional lands to the north. They knew the chance of success increased with their numbers—and by following this hell of an angry war god, Jehovah. They turned out to be right.

Jehovah's Rank

What do we know about Jehovah? He was referred to as one of the "Shining Ones." If we believe the Bible, he did indeed shine—and so brightly that mortal men could not bear to look him in the face. He was considered by the Israelites to be the leader of the Shining Ones, but this was not the case.

It says in I Samuel 4:4 that Yahweh (Jehovah) was first called "Sabaoth who sits above the Cherubim." The Cherubim was a group of the Shining Ones under the command of Gabriel, so it follows that Jehovah was above the Cherubim and on par with the archangels Gabriel, Uriel (aka Enki), Raphael, Michael, etc. Out of all the Shining Ones, those above this archangel group were Enlil—the Lord of Spirits, and Anu—the Most High. Jehovah was a somewhat high-ranking god, however, he was below Anu and Enlil and not the "leader of the Shining Ones" or "the God of gods," as the Israelites had called him (Joshua 22:22). This was Jehovah's power-hungry claim, as he attempted to bring the Middle East under his control through brute military force.

Other justifiable arguments exist which put Jehovah even lower on the hierarchy of the gods since he was an isolated tribal leader. In fact, the group he led was so relatively small that it did not even have a permanent home. They were a bunch of rag-tag vagabonds scrounging in the wilderness, fighting for the recognition of their god through warfare. A high-ranking god would command more of a following without having to fight for it, but I have given Jehovah the benefit of the doubt in the previous paragraph, and placed him as highly as he could *possibly* have been.

As time went on, many of the Israelites considered their own god, Jehovah, as having tremendous power over them, but also knew him as being totally ineffective against their enemies. Their Syrian neighbors also had Jehovah's number, stating that he was a mountain god with power in the hills, but was a real wimp in the valleys (if you don't believe me, check out I Kings 20:23 & 28).

Sex Appeal or Blackmail?

What made the followers of Jehovah worship him? What was it that made him so appealing over the other available gods like Baal? Apparently it was the covenant—the deal that was made between Jehovah and his followers.

A covenant is when two parties sit down and create an agreeable pact. We've all heard of the Lord's covenant with the Israelites—but was this really a covenant? In Leviticus Jehovah outlines this "covenant" by saying to them,

> If you follow my laws and faithfully
> observe my commandments, I will
> grant you rains in the season. . . you
> shall eat your fill of bread, and dwell
> securely in your land. But if you do
> not obey me and you break my
> Covenant I will wreak misery upon
> you—consumption and fever, which
> cause the eyes to pine and the body to
> languish.

Leviticus 26:3–16

This was no covenant—it was *blackmail!* He was stating "obey me, or else!" And notice he says, "if you break *my* covenant," not *our* covenant. The people had no say in this so-called "agreement." It was thrust upon them. Their opinion never mattered, nor was it asked for. So when you hear about God's wonderful covenant with the Israelites, just remember how much choice they had in the matter. The threats in Leviticus went on and on, and the quote above reflects only a small sample of these mean-spirited, Mafia-type tactics that were employed.

A Physical Being Who Flew in a "Cloud"

The power to enforce such an "agreement" goes beyond that of being a mere mortal. Jehovah may not have been the True God, but he was certainly *a* god. The ancients called them the gods, or the Shining Ones. Following the career of Jehovah provides insight into who these gods were and how they operated. Jehovah's exploits were documented far more extensively than those of the other early gods because his tribe was centered around him for a long period of time—from the flight from Egypt around 1200 BC to the end of the Babylonian Empire in 539 BC—about 640 years.

The first important act Jehovah performed was to lead the Israelites out of Egypt. He planned the departure, chose the route, and led them away. In Exodus 13:21 it says,

> The Lord went before them in a pillar
> of cloud by day to guide them along
> the way, and a pillar of fire by night,
> that they might travel day and night.

A pillar, to us and to the Israelites, is a support capable of holding up some other object. That is what pillars do. "A pillar of cloud" does not mean a cloud shaped like a pillar. It means a cloud-like object performing the function of a pillar—suspending itself in the air. It supported the Lord in the air—like a cloud—explained this way since the Israelites knew of nothing else at the time that could suspend itself in the air or hover, except for a cloud. Based on their limited technology, what else could they call this suspended aircraft but a "pillar?"

And at night it became a "pillar of fire," casting such strong light downward that the Israelites could follow its path over rough terrain.

I assert and believe strongly that Jehovah led them from the sky in an advanced aerial craft. I have immense respect for scholars who have put forth interesting evidence that Jehovah was actually a volcano and worshipped as a volcano god, but I favor the aerial craft theory, with Jehovah being an actual entity. The Bible says Jehovah "*went* before them in a pillar of cloud by day to guide them along the way,. . ." suggesting that Jehovah actually moved, physically, out ahead of the Israelites in order to guide them. A volcano does not physically travel anywhere.

". . .and a pillar of fire by night, that they might travel day and night," also suggests that the Israelites were on a long journey. If they spent a full day travelling away from a volcano, they certainly could not use its light by the time nighttime came—unless, of course, this light was travelling *with* them. The gods were not forces of nature, as many would have us believe.

I disagree with such theories only to show that the gods were really here, on this earth, and possessed advanced technological powers. Jehovah, unlike many other gods, misused those powers and mistreated his people.

The only way the subsequent atrocities committed by Jehovah make any sense is in the context of him being a supernatural entity. And the most logical type of supernatural entity there is, based on our evidence, is an extraterrestrial. Extra means "more than," or "beyond," and terrestrial means "the earth." So an extraterrestrial is from beyond the earth. If that is the case, such a supernatural creature would need some sort of advanced form of travel to get here. The best way for a person from Old Testament times to describe such a craft might easily be a "pillar of cloud," or a "pillar of fire."

Such a description was not unique in ancient times, as many similar sightings did occur. The Egyptians refer to something called the "Eye of Horus" hovering over the Pharaoh as protection, and centuries earlier than Yahweh/Jehovah, Thutmose III of Egypt mobilized his army after "fiery circles" appeared in the sky over the capital city.

Found in India's sacred books are stories of flying chariots in ancient times called vimanas, used by the gods for travel and warfare. Even cave paintings by ancient man show objects in the sky that resemble the flying saucers of today to an incredible degree. The point is that the gods, including Jehovah, were supernatural-type beings from beyond this earth that were here for a time.

Scientists have determined that the chance for advanced forms of intelligent life in the universe is so high that one would be a fool to believe otherwise. The two stars in Zeta Reticuli, for example, are similar to our sun and could easily support planets like the earth—but were in existence for one million years before we were. Given a million-year head start, or even 10,000 years, we cannot even imagine the technology that an advanced culture would have over us. I am not stating that this is where Jehovah or the gods came from, it merely serves as one example out of millions of similar possibilities. We must also remember that although cultures with higher technological prowess may exist, that does not necessarily translate into higher moral or ethical conduct.

The Art of Coercion

It seems Jehovah, due to his own shortcomings and personality deficiencies, was not sure how to relate to his followers aside from using brute force. One thing is certain, however. His methods were effective. By the time they reached Mt. Sinai, the Israelites were totally dependent upon him. Shortly thereafter, Jehovah's power trip kicks into high gear and cruelty surfaces on a number of levels.

In Exodus 19:12-13 he says,

> Whosoever toucheth the mountain shall be surely put to death; There shall not a hand touch it, but he shall surely be stoned, or shot through; whether it be beast or man, it shall not live,. . .

In other words, Jehovah wanted to control his people totally, but did not want them coming near him or the mountain he was on, except for Moses (and on rare occasions others, when invited).

Shortly following this, Jehovah makes his covenant with his people. He makes a multitude of great sounding promises to them. Should they obey his commandments, he will grant them rains for crops, all kinds of food, peace in the land, power over enemies, and blessings of fertility. Just obey him, that's all. But obey him to the "t." Don't even make one little mistake, cuz if you do and end up not obeying, you're in really deep—well, trouble. In Leviticus he says to his people,

> If you do not observe all my com-
> mandments and you break my
> covenant [note he does not say "our"
> covenant], I will in turn do this to
> you: I will wreak misery upon you—
> consumption and fever, which cause
> the eyes to pine and the body to lan-
> guish; you shall sow your seed to no
> purpose, for your enemies shall eat it.
> I will set my face against you, you
> shall be routed by your enemies, and
> your foes shall dominate you. You
> shall flee though none pursues.
>
> *Leviticus 26:15–16*

And this is just the beginning! He says if they still do not obey him he will punish them seven times over for their sins, dry up all the land, loose wild beasts upon them that will eat their children and wipe out their cattle, bring sword against them, cause pestilence and death—you name it—he was ready and willing to do to them every evil thing that you could imagine. Apparently, Jehovah had so much fun doing this to the Egyptians that he put his own people next in line.

The agreement governing this was not a freely negotiated one. If it was, I'm sure the Israelites would have objected to the severity of some (if not all) of these points. Any intelligent society would never have accepted such terms—consisting of being reduced to cannibalism as a result of hunger, killing of children by wild beasts, pestilence, and desolation of the country. Simply for not following Jehovah's orders. And such terrible things did in fact result from people not following his commands—even if they broke the commands by *accident!* Some examples will soon follow but for now, let us continue with how the Israelites got stuck with a terrible, no-win deal.

This covenant or agreement was made so that the Israelites (in following Jehovah's orders) were to serve as Jehovah's troops in an effort to overthrow and control the entire Near East. However, this is something the Israelites were never told. Jehovah neglected to share his plans with them, as to how they would be used.

Compassion and love play a big part in the world's major religions, but no compassion or love was found for innocent people, including the children, when it came to Jehovah's law. If one person transgressed, *all* would suffer terribly. Jehovah was an impatient and angry god.

At one point the Israelites were said to cry out in the wilderness, "Yahweh [Jehovah] hates us!" Now why would a people choose to worship a brutal god that hated them? It seems at this point, they had no choice, after seeing Jehovah's power over them. It was far too late at this point, leaving them nothing to do except wail and bemoan their fate.

Jehovah killed people just for looking at his face. He said, "...you cannot see my face; for men may not see me and live." He does not say, "men *will* not see me and live," he says, "men *may* not see me and live." This implies giving permission, rather than it being some kind of natural law. This was not a natural law. Jehovah did not have some kind of magical face that knocked people dead when they saw it. People looked at Jehovah's face, then *he* knocked them dead. As the Bible shows, he did not hesitate to kill those who even accidentally saw his face. This reminds one of the heinous criminal who's known to have committed terrible crimes, then gets recognized in public for who he really is. The same result can be expected.

Two

TOTAL CONTROL

He who endeavors to control the mind by force is a tyrant, and he who submits is a slave.

—Robert Ingersoll

Old Testament descriptions of Jehovah have provided a field day for UFO writers, and for good reason. Jehovah traveled through the sky in what appears to have been a noisy, smoking aircraft.

—William Bramley

Beware of the man whose god is in the skies.

—George Bernard Shaw

It is clear that Jehovah was an actual human-type personage. He requested a large insulated tent built for him during their desert travels that included a "dining" table which was supplied with utensils and fresh food. The tent was said to also supply a place to rest and to confer with Moses. Judging from the measurements, one thing was clear about Jehovah: he was of enormous size—at least eight feet tall and, more likely, up to thirteen feet in height!

Remember the Bible quote saying, "There were giants on the earth in those days."? Jehovah was one of them. His size alone would create fear in any of us today.

Jehovah needed a tent (called the Tabernacle). He wanted to get out of his cramped "pillar of cloud" every so often. Was this "cloud" an advanced craft of some kind—a UFO? Read from the Bible and decide for yourself:

> On the day that the Tabernacle was set up, the cloud covered the Tabernacle, the Tent of the Pact; and in the evening it rested over the Tabernacle in the likeness of fire until morning. It was always so: the cloud covered it, appearing as fire by night. And whenever the cloud lifted from

Elijah, just before he is taken up to Heaven in a "chariot of fire."

the tent, the Israelites would set out
accordingly; and at the spot where the
cloud settled, there the Israelites
would make camp . . . Day or night,
whenever the cloud lifted, they would
break camp.

Numbers 9:15-21

What were they following? Their Lord was within this "cloud,"
so doesn't it seem reasonable that it was a solid object? It was an
object that could float, hover, and move in the sky—so that the
people could follow it. These followers did not know what this
cloud was. To them, it was an unidentified object that flew, which
they called a "cloud." Their lack of technology left them no other
explanation.

Keeping the Tribe in Line

Jehovah was in possession of high technology and, if he chose
to, could use it in negative ways. He was an advanced being, quite
large, with supernatural powers in his own right. He did not hesitate to use them.

Aaron was the chief of Jehovah's household (head slave). He
and his sons were in charge of cooking for the Lord, among other
things. Aaron's sons, Nadab and Abihu, were Jehovah's first murder victims on the day that Jehovah's tent was being set up.

There was a big celebration occurring and the two sons
attempted to please Jehovah by offering burnt incense. Apparently,
Jehovah did not like that particular fragrance and, since he had not
requested this well-meaning act, killed them both with a "consum-
ing fire." (Leviticus 10:1-2)

This put a damper on the celebration, to say the least. Moses
was left to do the dirty work by trying to explain to the grieving
Aaron why such an atrocity happened. He does so, from Jehovah's
perspective, by saying,

Through those near me I show myself
holy, [meaning Jehovah] and assert
my authority before the people.

Leviticus 10:3

Holy? Holy?? Excuse me, but no god becomes holy by murdering people. At least none that I worship. If this kind of thing is
"holy" I wouldn't want any part of it. Aaron, however, who just
watched his two sons roast to death, kept his mouth shut—probably assuming, rightly, that he would be next if he objected.

In fact, Moses did inform Aaron that he (Aaron) was under the threat of death in Leviticus 10:6. Then Jehovah shows up and the first thing he does is confirm it by threatening Aaron and his (remaining) sons, telling him that he or his sons should not drink any wine or ale before entering the meeting tent, or they're as good as dead.

A fine way to greet a grieving family. Talk about kicking someone when they're down!

They now spend 11 months at Mt. Sinai, training for warfare. Once done they set out, following the "cloud." After 3 solid days of marching the people complained, so Jehovah burnt one end of the camp with his "fire"—but we are not told how many were killed.

Then, at a place called Kibroth-hattaavah the people had little food, except for a bread-like substance called manna, so complained of hunger, weakness, and malnutrition. Moses went to Jehovah on behalf of the people and complained to him once again. They wanted meat and nourishment, something nutritious. Moses also complained to the Lord about the heavy burden he had of trying to keep all these people happy. It was a big job for one man, and Moses did not want to take the blame for these types of shortcomings, especially if they should continue. The Israelites were being mistreated by Jehovah and wanted some changes.

The Lord gave Moses his answer by saying,

> Gather for Me seventy of Israel's elders of whom you have experience as elders and officers of the people, and bring them to the Tent of Meeting and let them take their place with you. I will come down and speak with you there, and I will draw upon the spirit that is on you and put it on them; they shall share the burden of the people with you, and you shall not bear it alone. And say to the people: "Be ready tomorrow and you shall eat meat, for you have kept whining before the Lord and saying, 'If only we had meat to eat! Indeed, we were better off in Egypt!'"
>
> The Lord will give you meat and you shall eat. You shall eat not one day, not two, not even five days or twenty,

but a whole month, until it comes out
of your nostrils and becomes loath-
some to you. For you have rejected
the Lord who is among you, by whin-
ing to Him and saying, 'Oh, why did
we ever leave Egypt?'

Numbers 11:16-20, Jewish Torah

Jehovah stated that he would "come down" to the meeting tent,
implying that he was up in his aerial craft during this conversation.

So how did the actual conversation take place? It seems this
was done with what was referred to as the *Urim and Thummim*,
which some credible researchers believe were communication
devices found in Aaron's breastplate (Aaron, once again, was
Jehovah's chief servant or "errand boy," which would make communication with him important).

When read carefully, the tone of Jehovah's entire response to
the request for better food is reminiscent of childish vindictiveness. Most *people* have matured far past this mindset, and here we
have a "god" displaying it.

Jehovah did in fact come down and "blessed" the people with
enough quail to make them sick of eating them. But Jehovah could
not wait for the people to tire and grow sick from the quail. With
the meat "still between their teeth," the Lord struck the people
down with a severe plague. Many died. An exact number is not
recorded but the place was thereafter named Kibroth-hattaavah,
meaning "the graves of craving." These poor people died merely
for the sin of being hungry. Jehovah had promised them a land
flowing with the abundance of milk and honey, but when they
complained of being malnourished from eating nothing but manna,
he got pissed off and killed a bunch of them. If Jehovah was the
infinite, loving God that we're supposed to accept, he should have
had no problem supplying his people with decent food and water.

But a pattern was beginning here. Jehovah would constantly
create situations like this whereby people would complain or break
a "rule," just so he could punish them. It was his favorite game; he
reveled in it.

Twice in the previous quote we hear the people stating that they
were better off as slaves in Egypt. If they knew what waited ahead,
it seems many would never have left Egypt to go with this tyrant
Jehovah. Defections and rebellions occurred continually against
Jehovah (see I Kings 11:33, II Kings 17:9-12, Judges 2:12 & 10:6,
Exodus 32:4, Jeremiah 7:17 & 31, Jeremiah 44:15,17, 23 and 25 to
name just a few). In fact, in Jeremiah 44:17-18 we find Jeremiah

trying to convince Israelites to return to Jehovah who had fled *back* to Egypt (escaping Assyrians). They tell him, "Why should we?" They say when they burned incense, baked cakes, and gave drink offerings to the Queen of Heaven, they were happy and prosperous. And when they ceased to do so, "we have wanted all things and have been consumed by the sword and by the famine." So why would they even consider going back to Jehovah? That's like a battered wife returning to an abusive husband. What for?

While in the wilderness, it became clear to the Israelites that they were better off as slaves. Yet today many Jewish people revere Jehovah/Yahweh as this savior-type god who "saved" them from slavery. Ha! They became even bigger slaves to a god that treated them horribly. And they were sorry for it when it happened.

Jehovah was not very happy to discover that the various defections and rebellion had led back to his own door (see below). Ezekiel describes being brought to the house of the Lord:

> Then he brought me to the door of the
> gate of the Lord's house which was
> toward the north; and behold, there
> sat women weeping for Tammuz.
> Then said he unto me, "Hast thou
> seen this, O son of man? Turn thee
> yet again, and thou shalt see greater
> abominations than these." And he
> brought me into the inner court of the
> Lord's house, and, behold, at the door
> of the temple of the Lord, between
> the porch and the altar, were about
> five and twenty men, with their backs
> toward the temple of the Lord, and
> their faces toward the east; and they
> worshipped the sun toward the east.

Ezekiel 9:14-16

Let's examine this. According to Ezekiel's vision, he was brought into an "other-worldly" scenario during this experience. It seems he was not at a normal temple of the Lord, but the Lord's actual dwelling place (or possibly the otherworldly place for those to worship him). If you had a burning desire, in fact, a vested interest to discover something about a well-known person, what would you do? You would probably go to their house. If you want answers you go to the source. When Ezekiel winds up at the house of the Lord, he finds people on his doorstep who have chosen to look the other way and worship the *sun* instead of Jehovah. What does this tell you? These people took the time to investigate, and *not one* of them was seen to be worshipping Jehovah. The Israelites, however, were stuck with him.

Making an Example Out of Those with Common Sense

Not long after the quail episode Jehovah executed 10 dissenting Israelites in front of all the others. These 10 were part of a group who scouted the Canaanites and their holdings, since Jehovah had led them to the area and had promised this land to them. Yet they found the Canaanites to be far more numerous and powerful than anticipated, and these 10 Israelites advised the others against attacking.

Jehovah was forced to compromise and wait for the next generation to grow up in the harsh desert—tougher, hardier, and more prone to fight. Jehovah would eventually be getting a better deal, but the current Israelites had failed his "test," and the main dissenters were executed as an example to the others.

At first, Jehovah was so angry he threatened to kill the entire group of Israelites—everyone. Moses talked him out of it, saying the Canaanites would hear about it and think Jehovah gave up, chickened out, whatever you want to call it, after seeing the deck stacked against him. Jehovah, not wanting to look like a fool, killed only a few people instead.

Besides, there would be plenty more chances to kill lots of Israelites later—all Jehovah needed was a half-assed excuse or two. In fact, here's a good example that soon followed.

Kangaroo Court

A couple of guys from the Reubenite faction, Dathan and Abiram, had assembled 250 highly esteemed Israelites to oppose Aaron and Moses. Big mistake. Some guy named Korah was also a ringleader. Korah, along with the 250 followers, were called to appear before Jehovah for a "hearing." This was, however, more of a sentencing than a hearing.

Jehovah declared, once again, that he would now destroy the entire community of Israelites except for Moses. Apparently, he loved to hear people beg for their lives. Moses and Aaron fell on their faces and begged Jehovah not to kill everyone because of something instigated by a few. Jehovah then told Moses and Aaron to address the community and tell them to "withdraw from the abodes of Korah, Dathan and Abiram."

So Moses told the community,

> "Move away from the tents of these
> wicked men and touch nothing that

belongs to them, lest you be wiped out for all their sins." So they withdrew from the abodes of Korah, Dathan and Abiram. Now Dathan and Abiram had come out and they stood at the entrance of their tents, with their wives, their children, and their little ones. And Moses said, "By this you shall know that it was the Lord who sent me to do all these things; that they are not of my devising: if these men die as all men do, if their lot be the common fate of all mankind, it was not the Lord who sent me. But if the Lord brings about something unheard of, so that the ground opens its mouth wide and swallows them with all that belongs to them, and they go down alive to Sheol, you shall know that these men have spurned the Lord!"

Scarcely had he finished speaking all these words when the ground under them burst asunder, and the earth opened its mouth and swallowed them up with their households; all Korah's people and all their possessions. They went down alive into Sheol, with all that belonged to them; the earth closed over them and they vanished from the midst of the congregation. All Israel fled at their shrieks, for they said, "The earth might swallow us!"

And a fire went forth from the Lord and consumed the two hundred and fifty men offering the incense.

Numbers 16:26-35, Jewish Torah

Those 250, who were toasted, were sympathetic followers of the ringleading families—the 250 "highly esteemed Israelites." In other words, all the intelligent ones who had figured out what was really going on had to be eliminated (before the word got out). This type of execution—roasting people alive—was fast becoming Jehovah's favorite. It was real quick and, much like the earth-swallowing trick (see page 82), required virtually no clean-up. He also loved the smell. The Bible states that the burning of flesh and blood created a sweet aroma to the Lord.

The next day the remaining people were up in arms over the deaths of innocent people (mainly children) from the families of Korah, Dathan, and Abiram. They had had enough, so approached Aaron and Moses with strong ideas of violence—that's right, bodily harm! Moses and Aaron had to run for it, so made a mad dash into the Tent of Meeting—that's right, Jehovah's tent (hell, where would *you* go?).

All the commotion caused Jehovah to descend and discover this unruly mob invading his tent—probably to his great delight. Here's an excellent excuse to kill people! Not being one to ignore a perfect opportunity, Jehovah reached into his bag of tricks and zapped his "chosen people" with a plague. Once again, something different, since you can get pretty bored murdering people in the same old way every time. This time, 14,700 people were killed. And if you don't believe this "all-loving" god could do such a thing, read it for yourself in Numbers 17:11-14.

This "flying off the handle" leads one to speculate on why the Israelites continually failed to follow Jehovah's Ten Commandments. What was the problem? Just follow the rules! The fact is, Jehovah promised them if they were to keep his commandments, he would live among them. I would not consider that a great incentive. In all liklihood they broke his commandments on purpose, just to keep him away!

> *If God lived on Earth, people would*
> *break out all His windows.*
>
> —Hasidic Saying

Jehovah All-Knowing?

We have clearly established that Jehovah was not an all-loving entity. But was he, in fact, all knowing? I'm afraid the poor slob falls short on this one, too. Let just one example suffice, since we could give you dozens.

This is found in Jehovah's explanation of a rainbow. He takes credit for making a rainbow back at a time when people had no idea, scientifically, exactly how rainbows are generated. The conditions existed for them to occur long before Jehovah supposedly came up with the original idea—which was immediately following the flood. Rainbows were around for a few million years before this, but he has no problem taking credit for it.

Jehovah states that the rainbow is a token for his covenant that says there will never, ever come a time when the earth is again destroyed by a flood (sounds wonderful, Jehovah, but what about fire, bombs or diseases?). He states that this covenant will last for "perpetual generations." An everlasting covenant. The rainbow, he says, is meant to remind him of this covenant.

> And the bow shall be in the cloud;
> and I will look upon it, that I may
> remember the everlasting covenant
> between God and every living crea-
> ture of all flesh that is upon the earth.

Genesis 9:16

If something is perpetual (like perpetual motion), then it happens automatically. What do you need to remember it for? And if Jehovah is all knowing, why would he need to "remember" his covenant? He should already know it!

Not only that, only a psychopath would require a reminder to keep from killing millions of people. Can you just picture Jehovah getting ready to cause another great flood, having forgotten the last one (probably insignificant to him), and needing a *reminder* that says, "Hold up a minute, there's that's rainbow I made! Man, I'm glad I saw that. I was ready to fly off the handle and kill another few million innocent people. But this rainbow I made tells me not to do it this time." Otherwise, we're all dead meat. Jehovah, all knowing? I don't think so.

Jehovah's Advanced Leadership Program

Let's take a look at how Jehovah rewarded both Moses and Aaron for their long years of leadership and good service to their god.

It is now a generation later, after the time Jehovah backed down from entering Canaan, so he again leads his people back to the area. With little water in the parched desert, the people complain to Moses and Aaron of thirst. Jehovah intervenes to provide water, telling Moses and Aaron to strike a certain rock with a rod and water will spring forth.

Before Moses strikes the rock he asks the people, "Shall we get water for you out of this rock?" He strikes the rock and it happens! But because Moses had put this in the form of a question, Jehovah punishes both Moses and Aaron for not trusting in his power enough, by excluding them from entering into the chosen land.

Jehovah orders Moses to bring Aaron and his son Eleazar up to Mount Hor. Moses strips Aaron of his garments, puts them on his son and leaves Aaron naked, to die on the mountain—which he does. So much for being Jehovah's faithful servant.

I cannot conceive of a God who
rewards and punishes his creatures,
or has a will of the kind that we expe -
rience in ourselves.

—Albert Einstein

His right-hand man, Moses, after so many years of toil and hardship, is also excluded from entering the Promised Land. A new and younger leader, Joshua, is eventually chosen but for now, until they actually get to Canaan's doorstep, Moses is allowed to retain his leadership. They win some important military battles in this way and indeed reach Canaan's doorstep, encamped now with friendly Midianites and Moabites.

The Moab women invite the Israelites to partake in feasts held for local gods, especially Baal, and during this ritual Jehovah returns from an excursion to discover this outside worship. This is like the husband coming home and finding the milkman in bed with his wife. Needless to say, Jehovah goes through the roof. There will be hell to pay. Worshipping some other god behind ol' Jehovah's back just was not kosher.

Jehovah tells Moses to:

> Take all the leaders of the people. Impale them for Jehovah here in the sun; then the burning anger of Jehovah will turn away from Israel.

Numbers 25:4

So Jehovah not only wanted the ringleaders who had turned his people to Baal dead, he wanted them to suffer—and to suffer in the most unspeakable, detestable manner imaginable. Impaling was the most torturous death known, with the victim's full weight being fixed through the anus upon a sharp wooden stake, piercing up through the inner organs and sometimes out the mouth. Not only was the agony more terrible than you could ever imagine, victims would often not die for hours.

It seems, however, that these orders were not carried out—only because Jehovah's anger was turned to joy because of a distraction. The Israelites were wailing over this verdict at the Tent of Meeting when an Israeli man brought a Midianite woman (a Baal worshipper) over to his companions in sight of Moses and the entire distraught community. They headed for a chamber whereby the alert Phineas, grandson of the priest Aaron, followed them inside and fatally speared both of them in their stomachs.

Jehovah forgot his anger and became overjoyed with these gruesome murders, offering Phineas and his descendants the priesthood from that moment on. Finally, some of Jehovah was rubbing off on his people! He was thrilled. Thrilled enough to go from complete, blind rage into total elation—a "mood swing" commonly found in victims of mental illness. If you study history, one will find that Hitler and Stalin both experienced such mood swings. But at least, in Jehovah's case, it was enough to save many from a cruel and torturous death.

Soon after this, at Abel-shittim, Moses addressed his people in a kind of farewell speech. It was about time for Joshua to take control and Moses knew it. After a lifetime of hard work and devotion Moses was being cast aside like a used dishrag. He begged Jehovah profusely in Deuteronomy 3:23-29 to let him cross over with the others into the Promised Land. After all, Moses gave 40 years of his life and leadership to get them there—but Jehovah answered in anger, saying, "Enough! Never speak to me of this matter again!"

And since Moses now had nothing to lose, it seems he felt it necessary to blow the whistle on Jehovah, to remind his people of the sleaziness of their god and to clearly warn them. Which he did. Here's what he told his people.

> Should you, when you have begotten children and children's children and are long established in the land, act wickedly or make for yourselves a sculptured image in any likeness, causing the Lord your God displeasure and vexation, I call heaven and earth to witness against you this day that you shall soon perish from the land which you are crossing the Jordan to occupy; you shall not endure long in it, but be utterly wiped out. The Lord will scatter you among the peoples, and only a scant few of you shall be left among the nations to which the Lord will drive you. There you will serve man-made gods of wood and stone, that cannot see or hear or eat or smell.

Deuteronomy 4:25-28, Jewish Torah

Later in history this warning was proven correct in every way.

Jehovah didn't give a rat's ass about his "chosen people." Moses even *told them that*—maybe not in those exact words, but he did tell them, as seen above. During this same speech Moses gave as kind of his farewell, he remembered back to the time when the older generation would not march against Canaan. He reminds them that during this time,

> "You grumbled in your tents; 'It is because he hates us,' you said, 'that Yahweh [Jehovah] brought us out of the land of Egypt to put us under the power of the Amorites to destroy us.'"

Deuteronomy 1:27

There is no way that the Israelites could have won at that time. They were all virtually dead if they decided to fight. And if Jehovah was an all-powerful god, why didn't he step in and help them? He wanted to give them this land, didn't he? Getting to this area was the whole point, wasn't it? So much for an all-powerful god (to go with all-knowing and all-loving, previously covered).

But you know, Jehovah really *may* have been strong enough to wipe out those Canaanites, or at least help the Israelites do so. After all, he had thousands of ingenious ways to kill people. But what if he *did* help them? Then the land would be taken, the Israelites would move in and all the struggles would cease. No one would be left for Jehovah to frighten, manipulate, and move around the chessboard like a bunch of pawns. If he truly cared for his people he would have made them a home in this "Promised Land" at that time. After all, he parted the entire Red Sea to get them into the wilderness, didn't he? So what's the problem? He should have been able to transport the Jews into, and the Canaanites out of, the Promised Land in an instant—or at least in a few days. Performing a much lesser miracle (than parting an entire ocean) would have gotten them out of this cursed wilderness where they had suffered for so long. But he refused to help them escape from this terrible hardship.

He did not like them. Any of them. Look what he did to his two most faithful followers, as just explained. He left one to die naked on a mountaintop and coldly discarded the other one, who begged after 40 years to be allowed entrance into the Promised Land. A loving god? Get real. This guy did not even have a sense of morals, or enough kindness to reward Moses (who deserved it more than anyone), by allowing him into the Promised Land. The reason, I suspect, was that Moses was now too old to be of use to Jehovah.

Two bears maul 42 children in Jehovah's name

This was a mentally deranged "god" who hated his people. His treatment of them was consistent with hatred. When a group of children teased Elisha, Jehovah's prophet, he immediately "called down a curse on them in the name of the Lord." Two bears appeared out of the woods and mauled 42 of the children. (2 Kings 2:23-24, New International Version) It is often interpreted that the bears came directly from Jehovah himself. He also threatened to "spread dung upon the faces" of any Israelites who would not take him seriously. (Malachi 2:1-3) Would a loving God do something this sick and deranged? Find me something truly loving that Jehovah did in the Pentateuch, the first five books of Old Testament. Anybody. Please. Send it to me in care of the publishers. I want to know. [Ten years since first edition, still no takers.]

If Jehovah somehow did display any kind of love (it seems there were a couple of isolated incidents later in the Old Testament), it could not *possibly* come close to the hatred and brutal cruelty that he committed against thousands of innocent people.

Lastly, let's look at all the promises that were made. Jehovah promised his people many things. The big one, the important one, was the covenant. Made good by circumcision, it promised the Israelites supremacy over all other people.

Supremacy? In 598 BC the Assyrian King Nebuchadnezzar swept into Jerusalem, sacked the temple and its treasures and took King Jehoiachin back to Babylon as prisoner. Additional prisoners included the king's court, his wives, and ten thousand craftsmen and soldiers. Talk about welshing on a deal! Israel was supposed to be top dog over all nations, according to Jehovah. So where was he when all this happened? Who knows? Nebuchadnezzar certainly didn't, because he came back again in 586 BC and attacked Jerusalem again! This time he broke down all the walls, burned the city, and pillaged everything in sight. All he left was a pile of rubble this time. The destruction of Jerusalem was complete. He dragged away King Zedekiah, made him a prisoner, and then poked his eyes out. He took along the remaining inhabitants as prisoners and forced them to march over 800 miles to Babylon. Where was Jehovah?

Jeremiah had tried talking sense to the Israelites, telling them they would not prevail against Babylon by merely being Jews— they had to earn Jehovah's help through righteousness.

The Israelites, who still believed their God would never let them fall, denounced Jeremiah and tossed the poor guy into a dungeon where he almost died! When you're busy being brainwashed by a belief system, you have no time for common sense.

THREE

GOD OR DEMON?

*It was only when I finally undertook
to read the Bible through from begin -
ning to end that I perceived that its
depiction of the Lord God—whom I
had always viewed as the very
embodiment of perfection—was actu -
ally that of a monstrous vengeful
tyrant, far exceeding in bloodthirsti -
ness and insane savagery the depre -
dations of Hitler, Stalin, Pol Pot,
Attila the Hun, or any other mass
murderer of ancient or modern histo -
ry. We cannot have it both ways—
either God is indeed such a viciously
depraved monster or he is not. But if
he is not, then not just a few scriptur -
al passages but a very portion of the
Bible is wrong and on a question of
the most fundamental importance.*

Steve Allen

*Whenever we read the obscene sto -
ries, the voluptuous debaucheries,
the cruel and tortuous executions, the
unrelenting vindictiveness with which
more than half the Bible is filled it
would be more consistent that we
called it the word of a demon than the
word of God.*

Thomas Paine

On a number of occasions Jehovah seems to be nothing more
than an overgrown SOB. When the Israelites complained while out
in the wilderness that there was nothing to eat but manna—no
other food or water—the Lord sent poisonous snakes among them.
Many were bitten and died. Does this sound like a loving, compassionate God to you? Would this be your response to a group of
followers whom you loved?

The Question of Evil

The early Hebrews did not have a devil. All evil came from
God. God could not be the author of all things without being the

Jehovah, as described in the Bible: "There went up a smoke out of his nostrils, and fire out of his mouth devoured: coals were kindled by it" (Psalms 18:8). "Round about him were dark waters and thick clouds of the skies." (Psalms 18:11) "His head and his hairs were white like wool, as white as snow; and his eyes were as a flame of fire." (Rev. 1:14) "And his feet like unto fine brass, as if they burned in a furnace." (Rev. 1:15) "He had horns coming out of his hand." (Hab. 3:4) "And burning coals went forth at his feet." (Hab. 3:5) "In the midst of the seven candlesticks one like unto the Son of man, clothed with a garment down to the foot and girt about the paps with a golden girdle." (Rev. 1:13) "And he had in his right hand seven stars; and out of his mouth went a sharp two-edged sword." (Rev. 1:16)

author of evil. It was very logical to the Hebrews. God himself says, in the Book of Isaiah,

> I form light and create darkness. I make peace, and *I create evil*. I, the Lord, do all these things. [italics mine]

Isaiah 45:7

Could the language be more clear than this? A number of Bible characters don't hesitate to back up Jehovah's claim. Job said, "We receive good at the hands of the Lord, shall we not also receive evil?" If you know the story of Job, you can figure he had good reason to be asking.

Amos asks,

> Shall there be evil in a city, and the Lord hath not done it?

Amos 3:6, King James

Well Amos, who else do you think was responsible? There was only one good guess at the time, and Amos was making it.

So what kind of evils, committed by Jehovah, can we directly refer to? There were so many it's hard to know where to begin. What about lying? Jehovah was "the great deceiver" in his day (see below). Jeremiah, in praying to the Lord said,

> You have greatly deceived this people.

Jeremiah 4:10

So was "God" a liar? Yes! Jehovah caused the prophets to lie by putting a lying spirit into their mouths (I Kings, 22:23), so that the lies were Jehovah's, and not theirs. See also I Samuel 18:10. Elsewhere in the Bible Jehovah even admits to being a liar by saying,

> If a prophet is deceived, I the Lord have deceived that prophet.

Ezekiel 14:9

The Garden of Eden and the Father of Lies

Question: If the devil is the "father of lies" in the (later) Christian system, who is it for the Hebrews?

If the answer is not already obvious, let's look at the events in the Garden of Eden. Here we have Jehovah telling Adam,

Adam and Eve expelled from Eden

> In the day thou eatest thereof thou
> shalt surely die.

Genesis 3:3

He was referring to the fruit from the tree. The serpent (the so-called "father of lies") counters by saying,

> Ye shall not surely die.

Genesis 3:4

Seeing that Adam lived nine hundred and thirty years, who was telling the truth when comparing the previous two statements?

Now pay attention to this part: The serpent tells Eve,

> For God doth know that in the day ye
> eat thereof, then your eyes shall be
> opened, and *ye shall be as gods*,
> knowing good and evil.

Genesis 3:5

The serpent has told Eve exactly what will happen. God (Jehovah) then admits to the family of gods,

> Behold, the *man is become as one of
> us*, to know good and evil.

Genesis 3:22

Please go back and compare the italicized words from each quote, first by the serpent, then by God. God (Jehovah) is *admit-ting* that the serpent was right. God *himself* has *admitted* that the serpent told the truth. How can the serpent be accused of deceiving humanity in the garden of Eden when Jehovah himself has admitted that the serpent was, in fact, right?

The serpent in the Garden of Eden *was not* the devil. If you go to the Bible and try to find the first mention of Satan, it will be found in I Chronicles 21:1, and far beyond Genesis. No attempt is made to introduce him, nor is any attempt made to explain his existence in the Hebrew belief system of the time.

This first mention was written approximately 800 years after Moses died. The existence of Satan, or the deceiving devil, was added hundreds, possibly thousands, of years after the events supposedly occurred in the Garden of Eden. Once again, remember who was responsible for evil in the Hebrew religion (as already explained—Jehovah). Don't fall for the theological trick of pawning off a later creation (Satan) as the father of lies when, according to the Hebrews themselves, it was their own God, Jehovah. This is not propaganda. It is pure and simple fact.

How exactly did Satan become integrated, then, into the Bible? It so happened that Deva and Shaitan, the Persian names for the cause of evil, were transformed by early Jews into "devil" and "Shatan" (Satan). This happened at about the same time as the appearance of stories showing Jehovah changing into a "really nice guy." But *originally*, who was nicer—the serpent or Jehovah? Who showed compassion? Who really cared?

We would never have been conscious to this day if it were not for the serpent. We would still be blind, our eyes would not be "open", we would never even know the difference between right and wrong, or have the ability to gather knowledge, or to learn *anything*, if it wasn't for the serpent! Think about that for a moment. We would still be stumbling around as mindless slaves, toiling for the gods, unable to think for ourselves, if it wasn't for the liberating serpent. This serpent being, whoever it was (and it was not the devil), clearly cared about the human condition and was trying to do something to help. This behavior is the complete antithesis to what we normally find with Jehovah.

The Criminal Element

We've now completed the section on lying. Let's explore Jehovah's actual crimes, like robbery and murder. Jehovah sanctioned robbery in Exodus 12:35-36, where it was called "borrowing," and murder in Numbers 11:1, Samuel 6:19, Deuteronomy 13:5 and 13:9, and on and on and on. There are at least 61 different Bible passages that portray Jehovah as being either directly or indirectly (with his help or under his command) involved in murder. What would happen today to anyone brought up on 61 counts of murder? What kind of news coverage would that get? Such a person, to many misaligned souls, would be considered as a kind of warped "god." We've seen it happen with our most notorious serial killers, who have even developed fan clubs. Apparently, in Old Testament times, we find this phenomenon already at work.

Often times, Jehovah would murder *his own people* and *not* the "enemy." Even our worst serial killers would never stoop to murder their own friends or admirers. But to Jehovah this did not matter—his own worshippers were his favorite murder victims.

If gods do evil then they are not gods.

—Euripides

It always seems that when Jehovah had a full load of evil deeds to perform, he would contract out the extras to various evil demons. For instance, in Exodus 12:23 the Lord, it says, can choose to send a "destroyer" to smite you, instead of doing it himself. Apparently Jehovah only has time to kill important people, so if you're not some kind of big shot, he'll contract out his dirty work to some other local demon who could use a few extra shekels.

In Exodus 4:24 Jehovah showed up in person to kill Moses, but was talked out of it by Moses' wife, who said they should just circumcise him instead. Great. Moses gets to live, but I somehow get the feeling that he was still not happy about this arrangement.

Some of Jehovah's "contract jobs," where he sends evil spirits to do his bidding, can be found in Judges 9:23, I Kings 22:21-22, I Samuel 16:14, 18:10 and 19:9. In I Samuel 16:14 it says,

> But the Spirit of the Lord departed
> from Saul, and an evil spirit from the
> Lord troubled him.

If the Lord Jehovah had good intentions and was (is) good in every way, why is he *purposely* taking away a good spirit and replacing it with an evil one? Saul took steps to rid himself of this evil spirit, and succeeded—it didn't matter to him that it came from the Lord.

The Demonic Element

Here's one time Jehovah apparently showed up in person but didn't kill anybody. According to Jacob, all they did was wrestle.

> And Jacob was left alone; and there
> wrestled a man with him until the
> breaking of the day. And when he saw
> that he prevailed not against him, he
> touched the hollow of his thigh; and
> the hollow of Jacob's thigh was out of
> joint, as he wrestled with him. And he
> said, "Let me go, for the day
> breaketh." And he said, "I will not let
> thee go, except thou bless me." And
> he said unto him, "What is thy
> name?" And he said, "Jacob." And he
> said, "Thy name shall be called no
> more Jacob, but Israel: for as a prince
> hast thou power with God and with
> men, and hast prevailed. And Jacob
> asked him, and said, "Tell me, I pray
> thee, thy name." And he said,
> "Wherefore is it that thou dost ask
> after my name?" And he blessed him
> there. And Jacob called the name of

Jacob wrestling with the "angel"

the place Peniel: "for I have seen God face to face, and my life is preserved."

Genesis 32:24–30

Jacob wrestled with some sort of supernatural entity, first referred to as a "man" in verse 24. However, Jacob knew better, and was holding fast onto this entity in order to obtain a blessing (getting one from a man would make little sense). He received his blessing and announced, in verse 30, "I have seen God face to face, and my life is preserved."

So Jacob claimed he wrestled with God. And won. What does this say about a "God" who is all-powerful? Not much. In fact, while Jacob held fast, this entity said to him, "Let me go, for the day breaketh." Oh, really. It was commonly known (or believed) back then that demons were robbed of their powers by the light of dawn. Not only that, the entity attempts to conceal his identity when asked for his name by Jacob—most likely because he fears Jacob will gain power over him if he gets possession of his name. This was another widely held belief in those days—to get possession of a demon's name means you gain power over him.

This entity also asked *Jacob* what *his* name was. If this being was Jehovah, why does he not know whom he is wrestling? What does this say about a God who is all knowing? Also, not much.

We have one of two things occurring here. 1) This is indeed Jehovah, as Jacob claims, but Jehovah is exposed as a low-level pretender-god/demon—unmasked for who and what he really is. Or 2) Jacob has mistaken an insignificant demon for Jehovah. Take your pick.

"Now, come on!" you might say. "Do you really infer that the Old Testament god could in fact be a demon?" No, I'm not *infer - ring* that at all. I'm *telling* you that he was. Was Jehovah brutal, ruthless and cruel? In addition to what we have already covered, I will continue to give you examples. Are demons known to be brutal, ruthless and cruel? Yes, they are. Do we have a match here? Hello?

He [God] is a merchant; the balances of deceit are in his hand; he loveth to oppress.

Hosea 12:7

I propose that Jehovah is not only a demon—but the king of the demons. Why do religious experts keep blaming Satan for the world's evil when "God" (Jehovah) has taken all the credit?

> I form the light, and create darkness:
> I make peace, and create evil: I the
> Lord do all these things.

> *Isaiah 45:7*

Think about it.

With all the atrocities committed by Jehovah, it is easy to see why the Israelites had no devil. There was nothing for him to do. The Lord took care of everything. The key figure of the New Testament, St. Paul, said repeatedly that the devil is the Lord of this world. He also states in II Corinthians 4:4, that the god of this world has blinded the minds of those who do not believe in Jesus.

Now why would the real father of Jesus do that?—blind people to the message of His only begotten son who was sent here or came here to save us? Unless he was not the true God at all, but a demon and an imposter! Jehovah was a demon, and the god of this world. Paul had it completely right, my friends, and you could base this on the evidence alone, outside of Paul's strong Christian convictions. Regarding Paul, however:

> *There are a thousand hacking at the*
> *branches of evil to one who is striking*
> *at the root.*

> —Henry David Thoreau

What kind of "God" would give Moses the Ten Commandments, including "Thou shalt not kill," then turn around and later command Moses to go into the cities of Canaan and "Kill every man, woman and child. Leave not a soul to breathe?" Would you consider this moral? Or depraved? Another example of the same edict is found here:

> But of the cities of these people,
> which the Lord thy God doth give
> thee for an inheritance, thou shalt
> save alive nothing that breatheth: But
> thou shalt utterly destroy them;
> namely the Hittites and the Amorites,
> the Canaanites, and the Perizzites, the
> Hivites, and the Jebusites; as the Lord
> thy God hath commanded thee.

> *Deuteronomy 20:16-17*

"That's right," Jehovah seems to be saying, "forget about the Ten Commandments and go out and kill anything and everyone in sight. It's okay. Make sure to kill all the women and children, too. It's okay, because I said so. But if you come back and happen to pick up sticks on the Sabbath, you will be severely punished." This happened to a man as found in Numbers, chapter 15. Notice how compassionate and forgiving Jehovah was.

> And while the children of Israel were in the wilderness, they found a man that gathered sticks upon the sabbath day. And they that found him gathering sticks brought him unto Moses and Aaron, and unto all the congregation. And they put him in ward, because it was not declared what should be done to him. And the Lord said unto Moses, "The man shall be surely put to death: all the congregation shall stone him with stones without the camp." And all the congregation brought him without the camp, and stoned him with stones, and he died; as the Lord commanded Moses.

> *Numbers 15:32-36*

You have Cain who killed his own brother Abel—and the Lord allowed him to live. But look what happened to the poor slob who picked up a few sticks.

Anyway, back to the slaughter in Deuteronomy. Maybe Jehovah had good reason to order this incredible slaughter of all these various tribes. He states these people must die so

> ". . .that they teach you not to do after all their abominations, which they have done unto their gods; so should ye sin against the Lord your God."

> *Deuteronomy 20:18*

If you break any of the Ten Commandments it is supposed to be a sin. Killing is one of them. So Jehovah is telling his people to go out and commit terrible sins so it will prevent them from sinning. It's now become obvious that Jehovah never took a course in Basic Logic.

The law given to Moses stated, "cursed is everyone who does not continue in all things written in the book of the law to do them." So what does Jehovah do? He turns around and breaks his own law! He lies, he murders, and he condones stealing, to name

46

"I'll never pick up sticks again on the Sabbath, I swear it!"

a few—cursing *himself* in the process. This might explain why no IQ scores of Jehovah have ever been published.

Beyond Moses, it is Joshua who qualifies as Jehovah's number one henchman and killer. Joshua butchered all inhabitants of at least eight cities (Ai, Makkedah, Eglon, Hebron, Gezer, Libnah, Lachich and Debir) because the Lord had commanded it. This included women and children, numbering in the thousands.

The responsibility for the creation of evil rests with Jehovah. According to Genesis, Jehovah alone existed before creation. When he created the universe and everything in it, evil is certainly part of that. If there is a devil it follows that Jehovah created him, since the devil would be part of the creation. So either Jehovah is directly responsible for evil, or indirectly responsible by creating the agent for it. I propose, however, that the devil is nothing but a myth, created to "cover" for Jehovah and pass off the blame.

Now let's try another test to see if Jehovah really was (is) a demon. How about some Bible comparison? Let's compare the first few verses of II Samuel 24 with the first few verses in I Chronicles 21. That's right, let us become amateur demon-hunters—reach for that Bible! Hallelujah. Let's figure this thing out. If no Bible is handy I will paraphrase below.

These two sections concern the same story told in two different parts of the Bible. Each results in Jehovah murdering 70,000 innocent Israelites. In II Samuel it is the Lord who inspires King David to count the Israelites—in other words, do a census. Yet, in Chronicles it is Satan who "provokes" David to do so. It is possible that they changed it to Satan in the later version.

Jehovah gets angry because of this census and wipes out 70,000 innocent Israelites with a plague. These Bible writers (more like editors) decided to cover for Jehovah by making Satan the bad guy in the later version. This way, Jehovah can be "excused" for murder by saying it was inspired by the devil. But what they forgot to do was go back and change the version in II Samuel to match it. Poor editing job, guys. You blew it!

Or, or here is what could be the real answer. Question: did they *not* change it *purposely*, because these two entities, Jehovah and Satan, were one and the same? The names were simply interchangeable! Think about that one, since it could well be the truth.

The angry Jehovah then informed David (through Gad) that he had three choices for punishment: seven years of famine in the land, fleeing three months from enemies who chase them, or three days pestilence in the land. David could not make the choice, so the Lord made it for him—the three-day pestilence killed 70,000.

Aside from the instigation of the census, what kind of entity would give three gruesome choices of punishment to somebody, then use one of them (at his own discretion, after the chooser refused to condemn himself) to kill 70,000 innocent people? Without being told which entity this was, the Lord or Satan, and if you were given the facts and told to guess which was responsible for this terrible mass murder, which one would you pick? It would be Satan, of course—but the real murderer was Jehovah. This act is far more consistent with that of a demon than a god.

If the Bible is to be taken literally and is the infallible word of God, then each entity in each version of this story truly *is* one and the same. The names were interchangeable. That is what I believe, based on Paul's assertion of this world being ruled by the evil one, and on Jehovah's history of demon-like deeds. If Satan exists, then Jehovah is really Satan.

But let us say, for argument's sake, that I am wrong. Let's say that Satan and Jehovah *are* separate creatures, and that the second version of the story is the only correct one. Then we have Satan being the instigator who causes David to number the people. That's a pretty nasty thing to do, especially if he knew it would anger Jehovah so much that he would kill seventy thousand innocent people. It would qualify as one of Satan's most fiendish and dastardly tricks. Has the devil ever done anything worse? But if he *was* guilty of such a thing, was it as bad as doing the killing? Was it?

Question: If Jehovah is *not* a devil or demon, is he not as bad or worse?

So we are left with a conflict as to who actually provoked David to do the census—but there is absolutely no question as to who did the killing.

If Jehovah also did the provoking, then this *would be consis-tent* with his other actions. Nothing could be more cruel and demented than to cause someone to perform a certain act, then turn around and slaughter thousands of innocent people because that person performed it. All this truly is, is creating an excuse to kill people—just because he feels like murdering a bunch of innocent people that day (this is something he did quite often, in many other circumstances).

There is one last twist on these two versions of the census. We find that the numbers taken in the census do not match, but we are certain that they pertain to the same census. In the first version it says that the number of men who drew the sword in Israel was 800,000 and in Judah 500,000. Okay, fine. But in the second version the numbers were 1,100,000 in Israel and 470,000 in Judah. So who is right here? How can you get completely different numbers for the same census? We are faced with a difference of 300,000 men in Israel and 30,000 in Judah. What's going on here?

If we accept the Bible as being literally true, then we have two separate "inspired" writers presenting numbers that don't match. It has always seemed unclear as to exactly what Jehovah was mad about regarding this census, but it is quite possible that he was angry over numbers that didn't match! In his great wisdom, he probably decided to make both versions correct by killing off the surplus people in the second account to match those figures from the first! I am starting to believe that the Bible is literally true, after all.

Unholy Alliance: Jehovah and Satan

Let's move on and cover the treatment of Job. After a long life of faithfulness Jehovah "rewards" him with terrible torments, deaths of family members, severe attacks of boils, the loss of all possessions, and the list goes on and on. The Bible states that Jehovah entered into a league with Satan in order to inflict these torments on this good and faithful man.

Question: What if you, as a child, suddenly had your parents turn you over to a cruel person who harmed and tortured you? Wouldn't that be equally as bad as your parents doing the same thing? Since they sanctioned it, aren't they just as guilty?

Remember, it was not Satan who convinced Jehovah to do terrible, hideous things to Job—it was Jehovah who enlisted Satan! Isn't Jehovah equal to a devil or a demon? How much more of this stuff do I need to heap on you before you get the picture?

Are Jehovah and Satan partners? You tell me. After the Garden of Eden incident, God was said to have punished Satan by making him crawl upon his belly, on the earth, from that day forward. Yet later in the Bible, God asks Satan where he's been and the reply is that he (Satan) has been "walking about in the earth." (JOB 2:2) Okay. So Satan is now up on his feet again. What happened?

This is like a police officer who catches a bank robber and after he is sentenced, arranges a reprieve. The cop realizes how "useful" the robber can be for a lucrative "inside" criminal business. They can work together, like on Job. Nobody needs to know what's *real-ly* going on, but we'll go ahead and pull off all these jobs together.

FOUR

THE SERPENT, JEHOVAH, AND SATAN

One problem with Yahweh, as they used to say in the old Christian Gnostic texts, is that he forgot he was a metaphor. He thought he was a fact. And when he said 'I am God,' a voice was heard to say, 'You are mistaken, Samael.' Samael means 'blind god': blind to the infinite Light of which he is a local historical manifestation. This is known as the blasphemy of Jehovah—that he thought he was God.

—Joseph Campbell

If humans must be tested and judged, why shouldn't the gods?

—Wes "Scoop" Nisker

More questions exist about the Garden of Eden, so let's go back to it again. What the heck was Jehovah thinking when he put that tree in there, then told Adam and Eve not to eat of its fruit? It makes no sense. Didn't he know, before making the tree, that its fruit would absolutely ruin this "perfect" man and woman that he had created? And didn't he know that the result would be a perpetual, deadly curse upon the people of the world from that point forward? God is supposed to be all knowing. He should have *known* this!

The *real* God (all knowing and all-loving) would never have done this. It's only common sense. But we are stuck here with Jehovah, an imposter-God whose knowledge is either limited or terribly flawed. Hey, Jehovah! If you did not want the fruit of the tree of knowledge to be eaten, why did you create it? Why? If you did not want Adam and Eve to partake of this fruit, as you stated, why did you place it before them? What is *wrong* with you, dude? If you did not want your creations to fall under the spell of a terrible curse, then why did you make the conditions possible for them to do so? Would the worst *demon* there ever was be so cruel to actually enact and produce conditions that would inevitably cause unhappiness and endless suffering to millions of innocent human beings??

Doesn't the Bible say somewhere that God is forgiving? Of course it does! (in the New Testament) But Jehovah is *not* forgiving. Why? Because he is *not the real God.* He did not forgive Adam and Eve of their offense (or anyone else, for that matter).

> And Joshua said unto the people, "Ye cannot serve the Lord: for he is an holy God; he is a jealous god; he will not forgive your transgressions nor your sins."
>
> *Joshua 24:19*

We are taught to show compassion and forgive even the worst of sins perpetrated against us, which many of us do, but if our own god won't do it for us, then we're *really* in trouble. This means that before Jesus came along to die for people's sins there was no forgiveness at all and hell is full of souls who simply missed the boat. If you find an instance where Jehovah actually forgave someone, please write to me in care of the publisher and let me know.

In the meantime, we have these two new and inexperienced people in the world, Adam and Eve, who ate a small bit of fruit that Jehovah had created. Was this so great a crime that Jehovah could neither forgive them or their offspring after them, *forever*?

I tend to think that Jehovah expelled them from the garden not so much to punish them for eating from the tree of knowledge, but to prevent them from eating from the tree of life (there were *two* trees that were off limits in the garden). Jehovah even went so far as to station Cherubims to guard the tree of life and keep Adam and Eve away from it—didn't he?

If Jehovah really cared about his creations, wouldn't it have been better to allow them to eat from the trees of knowledge and life? What's the big deal? They would have attained full wisdom and defeated death—now *that* is a creation to be proud of! But apparently we were meant to remain "blind," and to perform menial labor in the garden.

The Serpent as a Hero

Did the serpent do an evil thing by inducing Adam and Eve to partake of the tree of knowledge? Did not their eyes become opened, so they could tell good and evil apart? Wisdom is knowing the difference between good and evil, isn't it? Is not wisdom a good thing?

So what is this "fall of man" business which is said to have taken place as a result of this eating of the fruit? Did this act throw man down from some lofty height, or did it rather not elevate him from a previous state of ignorance? Would you rather have wisdom? Or would you rather be blind and stupid?

> *Banish me from Eden when you will;*
> *but first let me eat of the fruit of the*
> *tree of knowledge.*

—Robert Green Ingersoll

Doesn't the Bible say that the "great deceiver" is Satan? Of course it does. But when it comes to the Garden of Eden story, who is the liar here? Jehovah stated that if they ate of the fruit, they would surely die. He even said they would die in the *same day* it was eaten!

In Genesis 3:3 Eve said that God said if they even *touched* the fruit they would die. Did this happen? No, it did not. And the serpent told them it would not. Instead, he said their eyes would be opened, they would be like gods, and would be able to tell the difference between good and evil. Did this happen? Yes, it did.

Question: What is wisdom? Didn't Jesus say, "Be ye wise as serpents." (Matthew 10:16)? This is something that Jesus encouraged his followers to be. Is wisdom evil? Or a gift?

Was the serpent's word proven true in the garden? Did he do a bad thing by inducing them to eat, or did he bestow a gift? Why is it that in virtually all other cultures throughout the world the serpent is revered and worshipped?

Do you think the serpent (referred by many as Satan) has been grossly slandered in relation to this circumstance? Who really told the truth here—Jehovah or the serpent?

By the way, the serpent was most definitely not Satan, just like Jehovah was not the True God. The concept of Satan came long after the appearance of the serpent.

Question: Any reader who finds a clear instance of Satan either lying or murdering in the Bible, please send it to me. I want to know. Does such a thing even exist with Satan? Enlighten me.

Did Jehovah Promote Life or Death?

If Adam and Eve had been allowed to stick around long enough in the garden, they would have become "regulars" at the tree of knowledge. In fact, after eating of the fruit, I suspect they immediately knew who lied to them (their eyes were now opened), so took a quick sample of the other tree—the tree of life—as they were being railroaded out of town. Didn't they each live approximately 900 years? (without the tree of life, how else could they have done it?) Subsequent generations, as attested in the Bible,

54

lived extremely long lives yet, as time went by, life spans became shorter and shorter because we were no longer exposed to the gift of long life. The gods lived long, including of course Jehovah, so a steady diet of this interesting fruit would and could provide everlasting life, or something close to it, if we should desire.

Adam and Eve were kicked out of Eden and denied access to the tree of life because Jehovah was dead-set against it—but living 900 years after a quick "eat and run" episode is pretty impressive.

As far as Jehovah was concerned death, not life, was the order of the day. He reveled in it. He continually challenged himself to come up with new ways to kill people and/or make them kill each other. This was theatre, and he had to be entertained in his own warped and gruesome ways. Would a kind, loving God announce, "And I will cause them to eat the flesh of their sons, and the flesh of their daughters, and they shall eat every one the flesh of their friend"? No sane person could think of a reason for this to happen, much less enjoy watching it.

Has Satan ever caused people to cannibalize each other? On the contrary, no. Has he shown himself to be fond of slaughter, cruelty, and vengeance? Has he killed off or destroyed tens of thousands, if not hundreds of thousands of human beings in an extermination program? Or was this the doings of god in the "great flood?"

Sure, Satan is known to be tricky and mischievous, but he never ordered thousands of innocent women and children to be butchered, and then had those orders carried out. Does anything in the Bible describe Satan as cursing and raving with anger at humans, and threatening to send down (or in his case, up) calamities and afflictions on the people? Or is this what we see from Jehovah? Think about it. That's all I am asking here—for you to think about it. If you count the people killed by Jehovah in the Bible and those killed by Satan it would not even be close. If this were to be used as a yardstick (and is a pretty good one, at that), the only entity qualifying himself as a devil or demon would be Jehovah.

At this point, fundamentalist Christians (if still reading) would say that I am possessed by the devil. I assert and know that I am not. But if given a choice, I would prefer to be possessed by their devil, Satan, than by the "god" Jehovah, any day. What about you?

Human Progress

Let's look on the bright side and talk about some good things that have happened in the world. Have they come from God or Satan? Most people will say that all good things come from God. It makes perfect sense, since we all know that "God is good."

But it is Satan who has been credited with providing us humans with most of the innovations that have proven valuable to us. When the printing press was first invented it was "of the devil." Why? It was bringing knowledge to the people. It was the intent of the Church to keep the masses ignorant; in fact they opposed the printing of any and all Bibles for quite some time. For example, John Hus was in large part burned at the stake July 6, 1415 in Prague for trying to make the Bible available in the native language so that people could read it and understand it for themselves. The Church has been doing this kind of thing for centuries.

General scholarship estimates that book burnings and repression of knowledge by the Church has set us back about 2000 years, intellectually. For example, another great discovery we experienced was in the sixth century BCE when Pythagoras put forth the idea that the earth rotated around the sun. Around 270 BCE a Greek astronomer named Aristarchus went further and proved the sun was a gigantic body and that the Earth revolved around it. He did so with an ingenious method of timing the half-moons. This was accepted knowledge for a few centuries, until the Church came along. Without the turmoil of the Dark Ages and its resulting repression, this idea could have grown and flourished. Instead, we lost this knowledge almost completely and it did not resurface until the 16th century (about 2000 years later) through Copernicus, who was persecuted by the Church for reintroducing it.

In the 3rd century BCE we had another great discovery. The accurate circumference of the Earth had been determined and measured by Eratosthenes, who was the librarian at Alexandria. But the entire library was burned by Christians in 389 CE. In the 8th century a bishop named Virgilius tried to reintroduce and promote the idea that the earth was round. He was forced to recant. When Columbus sailed to America, he was without this scientific knowledge. He did not know for certain that the earth was round, and many sailors of the day feared it was flat and that they might fall off the ends of the earth. Discoveries of new lands were immensely delayed since getting an accurate bearing was a problem. We were missing this knowledge for about 1800 years.

Many such breakthroughs were suppressed and lost in the Dark Ages, or had been previously burned by Church authorities. The greatest thinkers of the world, the Greek philosophers, were also not immune. In Greek, the word philosophy means "the love of Sophia" or "the love of wisdom." From the fourth century, when Christianity took real power, to the sixth century, Christianity held Grecian philosophy in vassalage—in other words, they allowed it to survive in exchange for its subservience. In the sixth century an Imperial Mandate finally came down and the last schools of Greek philosophy were shut down. Gone. It was "the devil's work," and took centuries before it resurfaced. Fact: If it wasn't for Christianity combined with a few other Dark Ages problems like plagues and barbaric invasions, we could have gone from Eratosthenes to Einstein in eight or nine centuries instead of twenty-three.

Throughout history, the Church has put up a bitter and persistent opposition to astronomy, geology, biology, paleontology, and evolution. At various times she has also banned or prevented the investigation or practice of medicine, surgery, anesthetics, agriculture, the census, printing, gravitation, a round Earth, the heliocentric system, geography in general, life insurance, and the use of steam and electricity. In 1633 Galileo was forced to recant under the threat of death after he discovered and could scientifically prove that the earth revolved around the sun. This proof was suppressed for years because the Church believed that the earth was the center of the universe and refused to admit otherwise.

The aim of the Church is and always has been to keep people stupid and subservient. Without knowing what's really going on, the masses will all be quiet, continue working at their professions, and earn money to donate to the Church. Otherwise, if people smarten up enough, they will attain a degree of education that will overcome the ignorance and superstitions promoted by the churches which will, in turn, put the churches out of business. It's that simple. History bears this out when you look at the overall picture.

Jehovah wanted the same thing for Adam and Eve—to keep them ignorant and working at their jobs in the garden. They were created to be workers, and nothing more. They were originally blind to reality and could not think for themselves. Thinking for ourselves is what the Church of today does not want us doing. Adam and Eve were slaves. That is, until the so-called evil serpent came along and freed them. They were given knowledge, consciousness, and the ability to see good from evil. Books also do this. What organization burned down the library at Alexandria— the world's greatest depository of knowledge at the time? The Church. What group came to Central America and burned virtually all the books of the ancient Maya, destroying the incredible wisdom of an entire culture? The Church. Is knowledge evil? Or is it the Church? You decide. The Church has done many good things as well—but we should not ignore its faults, especially its suppression of knowledge and intelligence.

The spread of intelligence throughout the masses has been the crowning achievement of mankind, and had to be fought for with blood and passion before it could happen. The spread of intelligence has done more for humanity than all the superstitions and falsehoods that have been spread by priests and prophets.

FIVE

LET'S FIRE GOD

The Old Testament, as everyone who has looked into it is aware, drips with blood; there is, indeed, no more bloody chronicle in all the literature of the world.

—Henry L. Mencken

Live innocently; God is here.

—Carolus Linnaeus

Often times when one says, "He's bad," in today's world, it's meant as a compliment. In referring to Jehovah, let me clarify by saying that it's not a compliment. Sorry. Jehovah was one bad dude in every sense of the word, except in the "nice" and "hip" way often used today.

What's interesting about Jehovah is that previous gods from around the world were also considered overly strict and often bad, but then faded into obscurity. This same obscurity is happening today with Jehovah. In the past, gods who were overbearing and sometimes nasty included Jupiter of the Greeks and Romans, Fohi from China, Ormuzd of the Persians, Brahm of the Hindus, Shamash, the guardian of justice in Babylonia, Osiris, the stern god of Egypt, and Mumbo Jumbo, from African tribes in the western Sudan. Ol' Mumbo would punish women terribly for breaking tribal laws. He was powerful at the time, but today the words "mumbo jumbo" are used for describing meaningless incantations or rituals. If patterns of history are any indication, Jehovah will be joining Mumbo and the other cast of characters real soon in the Retirement Center for Obscure and Mythological Deities just down the street from Disneyland, with Mickey Mouse, Dumbo, and the rest of the gang.

The world will not stop spinning if Jehovah is sent into retirement. It didn't happen with the other gods and it won't happen with Jehovah. There will be no worldwide cataclysm in his absence, because he's actually been absent all this time anyway. And there won't be a vengeful "return of Jehovah," as seen in those Texas chainsaw movies. He won't crawl out of the grave like in "The Night of the Living Dead," and skulk around like a zombie, frying innocent people with lightning bolts. According to the

57

58

Bible, he's already done that—and has worn himself out from the centuries of abuse to himself and others. He should be retired. And if he isn't already retired, we should fire his ass. Would you keep someone around who's pulled all the crap that he has? Especially in the position of "God." Come on. He's got to go. The pope should hand Jehovah a pink slip and let him know that his services are longer required.

Jehovah seems *angry* about this suggestion! After writing these words at three in the morning, a huge pile of heavy boxes mysteriously toppled over by themselves in the garage, making a major racket. I ran in, what a mess! No worry, though. If that's all the power Jehovah has left, I think he's finished as God. Even Mumbo Jumbo could do better than that. Let's get someone in there who can at least explode things or do earthquakes.

News Flash!
Jehovah Relieved of Duties

Vatican City—It was announced today by the Vatican that the Judeo-Christian God, Yahweh (aka Jehovah), was relieved of his duties as godly overseer of the planet, according to a Vatican spokesman who has asked to remain anonymous. Reasons for the dismissal include abandonment of followers, gross negligence of duties, a previous record of war crimes, and basic petty jealousy. The spokesman said, "We humans have been pretty much left on our own for the past few centuries, so the Vatican is willing to step in and take over Godly duties. We can handle it from here."

Jehovah was unavailable for comment, but when pressed further as to what the deity might do, the spokesman said, "With the discovery of other planets, we estimate there to be primitive barbarian hordes on at least a quarter million of them. We're sure Jehovah will pick out the most violent and detestable bunch and move in on their planet. If not, we suspect he'll retire on a completely empty planet somewhere and continue doing what he's been doing for the past few centuries—nothing. He obviously needs a rest and with that being the case, we'd prefer he do it somewhere else."

Paul Tice, a Gnostic minister who got wind of the news announced, "I think we've proven that we're ready for a God of love, and would actually prefer that He take over, instead of the Vatican. Unfortunately, Jehovah has always refused to acknowledge a higher God, so it's doubtful that he would assist in finding the needed replacement." When asked what our next move should be, Tice replied, "We should look within ourselves for the answer, instead of to some outside authority. The true God can be found within us, but few people bother to look."

A young cardinal at the Vatican, who also requested anonymity, said, "We're glad Jehovah is gone. He was just hanging around expecting adoration and worship, but doing nothing in return. He was like a washed up rock star who just hangs out and doesn't play music any more. If you're not going to perform, we don't want you."

When we approached a local branch of the Jehovah's Witnesses and asked their thoughts on the news, a high-ranking official barked, "This is an outrage! We're keeping him on as our God. We always will, now go away. You always tell us to go away when we knock on *your* doors! Now beat it."

Surprisingly, there was no comment from highly placed Israeli sources, who seem to be taking a "wait and see" attitude. But at least one major newspaper in Jerusalem has been running the following classified ad:

WANTED: Compassionate deity with immense power, willing to work long hours with little pay in poor working conditions within a volatile and divided city. Must be a good negotiator, but able to win out and crush enemies when negotiations break down. Previous track record essential. Please, no history of psychotic episodes or dangerous behavior that could affect your own followers in a negative way—such behavior must be directed toward enemies only. Jealous tendencies also not desired. Nonsmoker highly preferred. No pets. Call (666) NEW-GODD. Ask for Henry or Mr. K.

Jehovah as the Creator?

Was Jehovah really the creator of this world, and even the universe? This is what it says in Genesis. Can we rely on this story?

On the first day of creation God divided the darkness from the light. He called the light Day and the darkness Night, so they were created and did exist, but there was not yet any "day" or "night" experienced on the earth at that time, according to the Bible. The light and darkness had been divided, but the sun and moon are not there yet. In Genesis 1:5, at the end of the first day of creation, it states,

> And God called the light Day, and the darkness he called Night.
>
> And the evening and the morning were the first day.

This second line only serves as a figure of speech or odd translation that marks the end of creation for that particular "day." For instance, in 1:8 and 1:13 at the end of the second and third days of creation it says, respectively,

> And the evening and the morning were the second day.

Followed later by

> And the evening and the morning were the third day.

And so on. The appearance of night and day happens later, very clearly on the fourth day of creation. In Genesis 1:14-18 it says, in part,

> And God made two great lights; the greater light to rule the day,
>
> And the lesser light to rule the night: he made the stars also.
>
> *Genesis 1:16*

So the sun and the moon had to "rule" the light and darkness before actual days began. Since days were not able to be measured yet during the first three "days" of creation, we must consider that these were not literal days. The original word, when translated properly, undoubtedly means much longer ages, according to Biblical scholars.

In accepting six literal days of creation, it was also taught for many years by biblical literalists that the Earth is about 6000 years old. When proponents of this theory are confronted with the tremendous age of the earth, they fail to account for the geological strata and other proofs like dinosaur fossils and carbon dating (accurate up to 50,000 years). The beliefs of a six thousand-year-old earth have been thrown out due to irrefutable scientific proof. It took many ages for the earth to take form. This is just one more example of the glaring stupidity that we, as intelligent human beings, have been forced to put up with from religious authorities.

So on the third day, just before the sun and moon appeared, we have a problem. God divided the waters from the land, creating the oceans and continents. In the same "day," we have:

> And God said, Let the earth bring
> forth grass, the herb yielding seed,
> And the fruit tree yielding fruit after
> his kind, whose seed is in itself, upon
> the earth: and it was so.

Genesis 1:11

What's going on here? When does grass grow in complete and total darkness? Without sunlight, how do trees bear fruit? On this incredibly long "day" of creation we have grass and fruit trees growing in total darkness for thousands of years. Only on day four, as shown above, did God get around to creating the sun and the moon. Without sunlight, what the temperature would be on earth? Nothing would live! There would be no water to keep these plants growing because it would have been *ice*, frozen solid!

Jehovah took credit for being the creator of the world. It's found in numerous places in the Bible. Moses supposedly wrote the Pentateuch since he was in direct communication with "God" and theologians tell us that every word he wrote was the exact truth. So we can assume that the details of the creation were shared with Moses so he could accurately tell the world of Jehovah's great achievement. Either Moses was an idiot who could not remember details, or Jehovah was a complete imposter who had no idea how to create a world or a universe. Or both. It's that simple.

These examples might be offensive to some, but they're logical. No person with an IQ over 50 would ever think for a minute that a blade of grass or anything else for that matter could grow on this earth without the sun.

The examples covered in this book are practical, rational inquiries, laced with a bit of sarcasm for the pure entertainment and education of the reader. That's all. I seek the truth, and will go most anywhere to find it. One must be willing to throw out everything, absolutely *everything*, that one is expected to believe simply because someone told you to, if personal insights or experience, combined with pure common sense, leads elsewhere.

> *It is said that a desire for knowledge lost us the*
> *Eden of the past; but whether this is true or not, it*
> *will certainly give us the Eden of the future.*

—Robert Ingersoll

Six

PERFECT GOD, OR PERFECT LOSER?

The devil thinks he is God, or would like to be God or regard - ed as God Himself, or he lets himself be deluded into this kind of thinking. He is so deluded that he firmly believes he is not delud - ed.

—Anonymous author of *Theologia Germanica*,
14th century German mystic

Wisdom begins where the fear of God ends.

—Andre Gide

We usually conceive of God as being perfect. Was Jehovah perfect? No. Was he a loser? Yes. He was a perfect loser. He didn't do much of anything right, as will soon be revealed. And when it went wrong, he took it out on his "creations," his own people, and punished *them* for it rather than doing anything to correct his own mistake!

The Art of "Perfection"

In the Old Testament we find at one point that wickedness had spread across the earth, so God "repented" for having made man— in his own image, I might add. In other words, he made a mistake and was sorry for it. Now what? The easy solution (that he always decided on) was to kill people. Just wipe out the mistake and start over. This time, he sent in a flood and wiped out everybody.

If he really cared about his own creations, his children, he would have attempted to nurture them and turn them away from their wickedness. Educating them with schools or teachers would help people to see the problem, or the error in their ways. This could create a solution, but *knowledge* was something completely unacceptable to Jehovah. Just look at what he did to Adam and Eve for eating from the *tree of knowledge*—he banished them! No, making people knowledgeable was out—it was far easier just to kill them or banish them.

If Jehovah had the knowledge to successfully wipe out an entire planet of people, he most certainly had enough smarts to share knowledge with the people, if he would so choose, and create some kind of education program. But it seems a written language had not even been developed for people to use at the time that all this happened. Jehovah, in his great wisdom, could have easily provided it.

Saving people in any way was a waste of time for ol' Jehovah. There was no scheme of salvation at this time. Are you kidding? Salvation? Why preserve human life or their souls? Compare that idea to creating a massive flood that covers the entire earth, destroys everything, and kills all living creatures. Which one would you pick? For entertainment value (rather than compassion), I'd pick the flood. And that's what Jehovah did. *He didn't care.* That's the bottom line. He did not care about the welfare and safety of his own creations. Granted, they had strayed from being good—but just look at the example they were given. Jehovah himself!

Jehovah was allowing his own godly "sons" to come down and cohabit with the daughters of men. Things got totally out of control, and look who was supposed to be in charge! It wasn't the daughters of men who saw that the "gods" were fair and made the first move. The Bible says the opposite, so the women were basically raped. This kind of treatment was not only condoned here, but continued throughout the Bible with Jehovah's blessing. So no wonder there was wickedness all over the place. It wasn't mankind that began the behavior. It was "God," Jehovah himself, who allowed it to start up to begin with. This "cohabitation" was okay with Jehovah, but when it got out of control and other sorts of wickedness began to bother him, the easiest solution was to just kill everybody. They'd come back later and clean up. So we had the flood.

If Jehovah was the all knowing God he was supposed to be, he wouldn't have had this problem to begin with. He was a failure.

Let's go back and see what happened in the Garden of Eden, to illustrate the point further. If Jehovah was all knowing, he would have known that his creation would not be perfect and that they would sin. He would know that he would have to drive Adam and Eve out of the garden, that the serpent would defeat his plan, and that the entire operation would be a failure. This leaves us with the question, Why was the garden planted in the first place? And what was its purpose? To fail? I suppose it was meant to test Adam and Eve. That is what some would say. But why allow your enemy to test them, and achieve a victory over you? Especially if you knew it would happen beforehand. If there was an all knowing God, it was certainly not Jehovah.

Why would Jehovah fill the world with people, knowing that he would drown them all anyway? Plus kill all the helpless and innocent animals that populated the earth and, as far as I know, not one of them was a sinner. Did the innocent animals of the world intentionally chow down on forbidden fruit? Hell, no! Why would a loving God kill millions of innocent creatures? It's clear from the murderous rampages he performed in the Old Testament (of people), that he is not the all-loving God we've been seeking.

It would seem that by this time, in the modern world of today, we are collectively starting to get a clue about the identity of God. The true God. The most intelligent people, who deduce things primarily through logic, cannot possibly consider Jehovah as God due to the barbarity of his actions and the almost endless, illogical inconsistencies associated with the idea. The most spiritual people, who use intuition and an inner guidance to connect with God, cannot possibly consider Jehovah as God due to the lack of higher spiritual values found in most of Jehovah's actions. The only people who could possibly consider him to be the true God are those who are still locked into a rigorous, dogmatic mindset, fundamentalists in the truest sense who are still too stubborn, afraid or unwilling to give it up. Tradition plays a strong role in this; so does pride, while an upbringing in extremely devout surroundings sets the stage. It locks the mind into a certain set of beliefs that even Houdini himself would have trouble escaping from. It does no good to fight or argue with such people, one can only pity them, feel some compassion, and possibly attempt to provide an alternative path without arousing anger or being viewed as offensive. Nothing can truly be done about anyone's chosen set of beliefs until they themselves are ready to start looking.

The world was much more backward and barbaric at the time Old Testament was written. Humanity has vastly improved itself since then and the *potential* to improve itself far beyond this is even greater. The only thing holding us back is, in large part, our stubbornness in clinging to extremely primitive and outmoded belief systems. Our intellectual sophistication is light years beyond what existed in the ancient Middle East. Back then virtually no one could read and the existing rampant superstitions and illiteracy was eventually replaced by the advanced science, logic and huge jump in literacy that we depend on today. It is high time we grow up as a species and leave behind the cruel and illogical foundations that have led us on an errant spiritual path for centuries. Our religious beliefs, worldwide and across the board, have the right to keep pace with all of our other advancements—otherwise we are destined to act in the same savage form that spawned these religions to begin with. To this day, for example, Israel and the surrounding area is in violent turmoil to the degree that it seems there is no end in sight—and this is no coincidence. All the blame cannot, of course, be laid at the feet of Jehovah and his believers, as the Arabs, who are the other half of the conflict in this area, have an equally violent religious foundation of their own.

The point is, having Jehovah around in our modern world just would not work any more. People often wonder what would happen if Jesus ever came back today. What if *Jehovah* was to come back? Well, we fired him from being God in the last chapter, so that would be the smartest thing to do. What would happen next?

News Flash!

Jehovah Cited!

Fresno, July 23— On Wednesday police in Fresno, California pulled a car over for speeding and upon checking the identity of the driver, found it was Jehovah. Forcibly retired as God not long ago, he has apparently taken to the highways, racing every-body and running numerous families off the road. When the officer ran Jehovah's plate number, he learned there was an outstanding warrant for the driver's arrest involving past war crimes. When he approached the driver and asked him to step out, Jehovah put the petal to metal and raced off into unsuspecting traffic. The officer gave chase, but as he closed in on the speeding felon, his steering wheel became red hot and melted in his hands! He was forced to pull over and watch his unit melt into a bubbling mass of tar. Backup units continued the chase but also melted into giant toasted cheese sand-wiches, while a police helicopter spun in wild, errat-ic circles, upside down for hours. Although this is the first time anyone has escaped from a chase involving so many pursuing vehicles, Jehovah's godly powers have apparently diminished with age. A detective involved in the case commented, "Compared to the old days, he's harmless. We just need to bring him in."

Jehovah will be profiled this week on the "America's Most Wanted" TV show, which will include his picture—taken from a dash-board police camera during the the time of his speeding citation. So take a good look. If you see him, take no action yourself but call the FBI immediately. He may not be armed but is considered dangerous, so if you have any information, make that call now. We need to take this guy off the streets.

News Flash!

Jehovah Spotted

Iowa, August 4— A recent tip placed Jehovah in a bar in Des Moines, Iowa, having a beer with Bigfoot. When local officers stormed in, they found Bigfoot passed out on the bar and Jehovah sneaking out the side door with his wallet. Jehovah has become so elusive that even Bigfoot was heard to remark, "I wish I had a video camera."

News Flash!

Nazi Hunter Spots Jehovah

Argentina, November 10— Famous Nazi hunter, Blitz Kreigelberg, was closing in on one of the last remaining Nazi war criminals in a secluded village in Argentina when someone brought to his attention that a strange character who looked like Jehovah was running loose in town. Upon investigating further and comparing a police photo from "America's Most Wanted," Kreigelberg put two and two together and is convinced that he's found God. "It's him," said Kreigelberg.

Jehovah, wearing a Hawaiian shirt and carrying a cheap beach towel said, "You must be mistaken. I'm here on vacation," before ducking into a run down TV repair shop on Third and Main near a McDonald's and Jiffy Lube.

Nazi descendents and relatives confronted Kreigelberg in the street, insisting that Jehovah was as much a mass murderer as Hitler was, so why wasn't he taking him in? A war crimes tribunal is currently seeking Jehovah, who was last seen in an inebriated state three months ago from a bar in Iowa. Kreigelberg and a small crowd staked out the TV shop and when the suspect emerged, he was questioned once again. Jehovah, or whoever he is, stated that he is working on a project involving a television screen that will measure 37 miles high. Asked what it will be used for, this Jehovah look-alike stated, "An announcement, of sorts."

Following this, reports have flooded in of Jehovah's Witnesses buying plane tickets to Argentina at an alarming rate, while local vendors in this small South American community are offering $500 admission tickets to "Jehovah's Big Announcement." Bounty hunters from around the world are also converging on the area.

We'll keep you posted. Should Jehovah be considered dangerous? Probably so, even while trying to keep a low profile. Based on the Bible, he has been known to put "hits" out on people. We find a "deliverer" named Ehud, raised up by the Lord himself in Judges Chapter 3, who goes out and commits a terribly graphic murder, telling the victim just before plunging a dagger into him that, "I have a message from God unto thee." (Judges 3:20) The Israelites later follow Ehud into battle due to his "godly" deed.

Another example occurred as a result of the first Passover, when a certain "destroyer" was sent on Jehovah's behalf to kill Egyptians in their homes (see Exodus 12:23). The Jews, his own people, could also become a victim of Jehovah's murderous wrath for making a holy anointing oil once made by Moses, per

Jehovah's instructions. If anyone made such a concoction, they would be immediately "cut off from his people," meaning they'd be cast into the wilderness which, in essence, was the same thing as a death sentence. The Lord gave Moses a recipe for perfume, with severe punishment for anyone who would copy it. Why would the infinite creator of the universe care if somebody copied his recipe for perfume? Come on, now, something just isn't right here.

News Flash!

> New York— Since news of the reappearance of Jehovah, world famous clothing and perfume manufacturer Calvin Klein has reportedly gone into hiding. There is no other information at this time.

If Jehovah was all knowing, he'd have known there was a heaven and hell—after all, as God, he would have created those places. But does he ever tell anybody about them during the entire time in the Old Testament? No. He promised no afterlife to any of his people, nor were there any warnings on how to avoid hell.

If you believe in an afterlife of some sort, this is not the God you're looking for. But what if Jehovah was right? What if there's nothing to look forward to after death and Christianity made up the entire concept of heaven and hell later on? The advent of heaven and hell no doubt saved Jehovah from a terrible PR problem. With the threat of hell and a devil, Jehovah became a "good guy" to believing Christians everywhere. He became more acceptable to people who were all too familiar with his brutal carnage. But by now we should be sick and tired of bailing him out with Satanic excuses and let the record speak for itself. There *was* no devil when Jehovah was around, so let's not go blaming Jehovah's crap on something that got made up later on.

All Powerful?

Was Jehovah all-powerful? You've got to be kidding. He led his people around for 40 years in the desert trying to get them to the Promised Land, attempting to fight strategic battles in order to win that land, and backed off on a number of battles because he and his people were not strong enough to win. There is even one Bible verse that states Jehovah feared the enemy! If this was an all powerful God, he'd have no reason to fear anybody. He'd have rushed in and stomped everyone in two seconds and immediately handed over the Promised Land to his people, and would have been done with it. To hell with leading your chosen people around, making them jump through innumerable, asinine hoops while suffering terrible trials for many decades.

And before all this happened, Jehovah hardened the heart of the Pharaoh who had the Israelites enslaved, so that the Pharaoh would be sure NOT to release his captives, thereby giving Jehovah an excuse to punish him. An all-powerful God doesn't play these idiot games. He would just come in and free the people. But instead, Jehovah sends in Moses and Aaron to perform magic tricks. Moses tells his sidekick Aaron to throw down his stick, which suddenly transforms into a serpent. The Pharaoh, who was supposed to be impressed, just calls in his own sorcerers who do the same damn thing without any problem. Even though Aaron's serpents swallowed the Pharaoh's (oooh, clever one-upmanship), we need to ask, Would an infinite, all powerful God who wants to free an entire race of people resort to having a few magic tricks performed by a couple of underlings in order to accomplish that? What kind of an idiot god is this?

I suppose you could say exactly that. He was an idiot. To prove my point, let's look at this whole "hardening of the heart" ordeal.

The Method of Madness

The big plan to free the Israelites, concocted by Jehovah, was to be carried out by his two sidekicks, Moses and Aaron. The original plan didn't work because it consisted of performing magical tricks that were not impressive enough to create the desired results—at least until the last phase of trickery kicked in. This was when Moses' serpent swallowed up those of the Pharaoh's magicians. All of a sudden, it seemed the Pharaoh was impressed enough to free all of the Israelite slaves. But Jehovah stepped in and "hardened the heart" of the Pharaoh so that he (Pharaoh) refused to let the people go.

This was intentional so that Jehovah could bring his underlings to the next level and create more intricate stunts to impress the Pharaoh. The next morning, Moses and Aaron confronted the Pharaoh at the river and turned it into blood right before his eyes, causing the river to stink and making the water of Egypt undrinkable. In a "my god is better than your god" pissing match, the Egyptian sorcerers went and did the same thing to the remaining water supplies of the country, forcing Egyptians (their own people) to dig desperately around the riverbanks in an effort to find water that would keep them alive.

Just as it's been throughout history, when it comes to religion and a battle between "gods," human life means very little. The Pharaoh refused to budge. The next big move followed. Jehovah sent Moses to threaten the Pharaoh with frogs. That's right, frogs. If you were an all-powerful God with virtually anything in the universe at your disposal, wouldn't you use frogs, too?

Aaron cast down his rod and it became a serpent

So Aaron waved his magical wand over the land and caused an infestation of leaping frogs to appear throughout the land. Just to show that they wouldn't be outdone, the Egyptian sorcerers rushed in to duplicate the amazing miracle, causing billions of croaking critters to infest the homes of every available family. This was a bit harder for the Pharaoh to take, so he called in Aaron and Moses and said that he would let the people go if Jehovah would just rid the land of the leaping amphibians. So the frogs were vanquished, but Jehovah (you guessed it) hardened the heart of the Pharaoh so that the Israelites were not set free after all.

Jehovah really liked the way Aaron was using this magical rod, and figured out a new trick. Now that the Pharaoh had changed his mind, Jehovah decided to have Aaron transform all the dust of the land into lice. All the men and beasts of Egypt were infested with lice, but that didn't stop the Egyptian sorcerers from trying to duplicate the feat. But in this case, they failed. Stunned, they ran to the Pharaoh and announced, "This is the finger of God" (Exodus 8:19), while itching profusely. In other words, they were now impressed, and openly admitted it.

The Pharaoh, now knowing that he'd been outdone, seemed ready to throw in the towel. But Jehovah was having too much fun watching everyone scratch and itch furiously from lice throughout the land. So he hardened the heart of the Pharaoh—and Pharaoh refused to release anybody.

Jehovah did this because he felt the immense urge to release billions of flies into Egypt just to see what would happen except, of course, into the areas inhabited by the Israelites. Because there were so many damn flies, Pharaoh sent for Moses and Aaron and gave his permission for them to sacrifice to their God in Egypt. But they didn't want to do this Egypt, so requested a three-day journey. It was granted, so Moses said he'd put in a good word to the big cheese, Jehovah, on Pharaoh's behalf so the Lord might rid the land of all those stinking flies. And like magic, it all came to pass. It was now time for Pharaoh to return the favor by freeing the helpless Israelites. But there was a problem. Don't tell me. The Pharaoh got sick? No, he didn't get sick. Jehovah hardened his heart and made him an obstinate bastard. Nobody went free.

This is a real mind game going on here, being played out in the same way a cat plays with mouse, having the time of its life, just before killing it. "Chances" are given for escape, but only enough for the mouse to go a certain distance before being brought back to suffer more for the sake of the cat's entertainment. This demented ploy is exactly what Jehovah was doing.

So Moses and Aaron are sent back to Pharaoh to announce that all the cattle, horses, sheep, oxen, and camels of the Egyptians will be stricken with a disease and die. Which happened the next day. And none of the cattle of the Israelites suffered from this weird malady at all. Pharaoh, now surrounded by thousands of dead animals, seemed ready to give in and free the people. But his heart was hardened and he refused. Fun, fun, fun. Jehovah rushed in with another assignment for Moses and Aaron who, at this point, were probably getting pretty sick of this. Surely they could see what was happening by now, but they still wanted to get the Israelites their freedom so decided to put up with this crap and just go along with it. What they had to do was throw a bunch of ashes up in the air so that all the men and beasts in the land would develop strange and painful boils. But since there were no beasts left alive from the disease that had just occurred, all the dead ones were *still* apparently stricken, according to the Bible. Jehovah was very thorough. When Pharaoh did nothing because of this, Jehovah threatened, then made good, on a huge killer hailstorm. So as it began hailing. . .

> He that feared the word of the Lord
> among the servants of the Pharaoh
> made his servants and his cattle flee
> into the houses.

Exodus 9:20

What? How would you like to have a bunch of dead cattle, with boils all over their bodies, running around inside *your* house? These cattle were *dead* already. Dead! If the Bible is the word of God, to be taken literally, then Jehovah was an idiot. The cattle that remained outside the houses were killed again, a second time, by Jehovah who apparently had nothing better to do but kill dead things over and over again. A brilliant tactical maneuver. Apparently it worked, because Pharaoh broke down during the hailstorm and summoned Moses and Aaron. He admitted that he was a lousy sinner, that the Egyptians were evil, and that the Lord, with all his brilliant maneuvers, was righteous. The people would be freed if Moses could just get Jehovah to stop the hail.

But when the hail stopped, guess what happened. That's right, Pharaoh changed his mind because Jehovah hardened his heart so that this cruel game could continue. Locusts came next, and stripped the entire land of its greenery and fruit so that all plants and trees were barren. Pharaoh promised freedom and admitted himself to be a rotten sinner again, so Jehovah sent a strong wind and blew the locusts away. But when Pharaoh changed his mind again, a great darkness came over the land for three full days. Pitch black. Yet the Israelites had light in their dwellings.

Now here's an idea. Think about it. Here we have the Egyptians in such total darkness that, as the Bible explains, they cannot even see each other. And the Israelites have light—lanterns, or whatever, that they can see with. Gee. . . what would you do here? It doesn't take a rocket scientist to figure it out. They're slaves, have light, and their masters can't see anything. Duuhh! Here's an idea. You *leave*. If you want your damn freedom so bad, there's no better time to pick up your belongings and go! Get the hell out of there. Everything's dead anyway. And there's no food. But apparently, according to the Bible, they decided to all stay there in a decimated land, with nothing left, so they could all sit around and stare at each other (because they had the light to do it with).

So at this point, nobody did anything. What's going on here? Well, this book is being written partly to document the history of stupidity, so please excuse my frankness along with how redundant this hardening of the heart stuff is (yes, there's even more). If there wasn't so much cruelty involved, this entire section of the Old Testament could be categorized as one giant freak show.

So Pharaoh calls Moses in and basically says, "Okay, you guys can leave now. Go on, get outta here. Just leave all your horses, cows and pigs behind." Moses comes back with, "Hey, wait a minute. We can't leave without our livestock. We have to kill it all for Jehovah because he likes dead things." So Pharaoh is thinking, "Oh how silly of me. I should have realized that by now." But Pharaoh changes his mind and suddenly tells Moses that the deal is off, and they'll remain slaves after all. The Lord had hardened Pharaoh's heart, even more so this time, to the point that Pharaoh threatens to kill Moses if he shows his face around him again (Exodus 10:28). Pharaoh is pissed. It seems to have finally sunk in that Moses may have had something to do with the nearly complete destruction of Egypt and it might be a good idea to kill him if he keeps it up. Moses even tells Pharaoh, "Thou hast spoken well," concerning this, meaning, "it's about time you smartened up there, jackass." In fact, nobody in the Old Testament, including Jehovah himself, seems to have had much brainpower.

Jehovah then tells Moses that one final plague will be administered upon the hapless Pharaoh and the Egyptians and that after it was done, the Pharaoh "shall surely thrust you out hence altogether." (Exodus 11:1) Meaning that both Moses and Aaron could expect, once and for all, to be thrown out on their asses.

So Jehovah instructs his people to "borrow" all the jewels, gold, and silver from their neighboring Egyptians because it's almost time to go. I'm sure they had every intention of returning

Jehovah orders all the first-born to be slain

it. They just needed to borrow as much as they could get their hands on for the time being. Jehovah had proven himself to be such an upright, honest fellow, how could we ever doubt him? They were just "borrowing."

With that accomplished, Moses went back to Pharaoh. It somehow slipped Pharaoh's mind that he intended to kill Moses the next time he saw his face, but if that happened the Bible would have ended right there and there would have been no Exodus. So Moses told Pharaoh (on behalf of Jehovah) that about midnight the Lord will cause all firstborn things in Egypt to die—including Pharaoh's child, all other such people, and even their beasts!

Now the Egyptian's beasts already died of disease *and* in the hailstorm (twice), then were covered with painful boils just for good measure, and now the great Lord Jehovah announces that he will kill all of the firstborn dead animals. A brilliant move. Apparently, this is where the slogan "beating a dead horse" came from. One wonders in this narrative what the great king of the universe will think of next.

It doesn't take long to find out. He hardens Pharaoh's heart. At this point, what else do you think he would do?

Jehovah didn't have to harden Pharaoh's heart over and over again. Without doing this, the Jews would have walked free long ago. But doing it allows Jehovah to continue to administer unspeakable cruelties including, this time, the murder of innocent babies for nothing but sheer sport or to satisfy his urge for cruelty. This is where the ritual began with taking the blood of a slaughtered lamb and putting it on door posts on the first night of Passover so that the Lord would know not to stop and kill the firstborn at a Jewish home, but instead "pass over" it. Celebrating Passover, to me, is nothing more than engaging in the celebration of cruelty toward our fellow man—and we must get over this! This isn't right. I'm sorry, I apologize to my Jewish friends whom I respect and adore in many cases, but I cannot respect or adore such a celebration. It's a criminal celebration because it celebrates the fact that, although some received life, there is also the murder of innocent babies going on.

If Jehovah was caught today and tried for these acts, he would go to jail as a baby killer and, in a non-sexual but violent sense, a molester of children. Even hardened criminals can't stand child molesters and will try to murder them in jail. The worst of criminals draw the line there, and do not tolerate other criminals harming innocent babies and children. So why worship a "God" for doing it? And then creating a joyous holiday on its heels? I'm completely at a loss on this one, other than to realize that in earlier times acts of such barbarism were more commonly accepted than they are today. But if we are to grow as compassionate human beings, there are some things we must reconsider in our more modern lives. I am not Jewish, so don't have any right to state these opinions in the name of the Jewish religion. But I *am* a human being, and state them in the name of humanity. How we treat the fellow humans we share the planet with is extremely important. It should be with love and compassion. If a certain people is a "chosen people" that's fine—if they uphold an example of love and compassion for other human beings. Then they deserve the label. Some Jewish people do this. Bravo! The god of the Old Testament, however, did not do this—often times showing no love or compassion for his *own people*, much less the Egyptians. This is not my claim, but is factually stated in the Bible.

Jewish people would undoubtedly state that they are celebrating life, not death, during Passover. But it is still at the expense of a murderous god who victimized innocent young children. You cannot celebrate one without the other, because the other (meaning the murders) was and is the *cause* for the celebration.

So did the Israelites finally go free after this? Yes, they did. From the Egyptians. But in effect, they became the slaves of Jehovah, because they had to do exactly as he said. And if they didn't, they were punished to the degree that *any* slave would be punished. Read the Bible. The only difference was that the Israelites were now nomadic slaves, rather than being stuck in Egypt.

News Flash!

Jehovah Captured!

San Diego, California—After an extensive, year long manhunt, Jehovah, former self-proclaimed "God" and creator of the universe, has been captured. Returning in human form has proved to be costly. He was wanted for serious war crimes by a worldwide tribunal, and his powers are almost completely gone, due to advanced age. During his year on the run, Jehovah was masquerading as something other than "God," after having been officially relieved of those duties by the Vatican. He managed to stay hidden for so long because he had disguised himself and/or worked as a priest, a circus clown, an animal trainer, Santa Claus, and a miserly begger. He's expected to stand trial and, if convicted, will serve out his term in an undisclosed location. While being led into the police station in handcuffs, throngs of demonstrators turned out displaying signs with slogans like "Exodus Stage Right", and "Where's Noah When You Need Him?"

God's Holy Perfection Protection

The Vatican in Rome, knowing what an embarrassment Jehovah had become, attempted to forge its own holy book in an effort to change Jehovah's overall perception. The Latin Vulgate, which contains the holy books of the Vatican, had undergone centuries of revision in an effort to correct the thousands of mistakes that littered it. In 1592 Pope Clement VIII announced it to be "untrue", had them all burned, then had it redone using, in part, a corrupted medieval version instead of the original fourth century source text of Jerome. This new Clementine version used intentional mistranslations ordered by the Pope "to support the peculiar dogmas of the Church of Rome." This new bastardized version went through at least five more revisions in the late 1700's, until we fast-forward to the Vatican Council I in 1869. Here, the Vatican announced, in their great wisdom, that the books of the Latin Vulgate were completely without error since they were "written under the inspiration of the Holy Spirit, they have God as their author, and as such, have been handed over to the church."

So if God wrote it (through the inspiration of men), how did all those errors get in there? Oh, how silly of me—what errors? These books are perfect and divine, just like the creator who wrote them. Yet, how fast we forget. In 1902 Pope Leo XIII appointed a Commission of Cardinals to amend the Vulgate even further! Wait a minute. I thought there were no errors.

Apparently still at work on this, in 1930 the Vatican International Commission announced it was going to correct a "mistranslation" of Exodus 20:5 (for more on this quote, see page 88), which has Jehovah saying,

> For I the Lord thy God am a jealous God, visiting the iniquities of the fathers upon the children unto the third and fourth generation of them that hate me.

The new, updated version they came up with:

> For I, the Lord thy God, am a God of loving-kindness and mercy, considering the errors of the fathers as mitigating circumstances in judging the children unto the third and fourth generations.

What? That's what the Protestant Church said—they chose to keep the original version. Scholars have gone back to the earliest available rendering to prove the accuracy of the first translation and what an outrage and embarrassment this "correction" really is.

In his brilliant work, *The Crucifixtion of Truth* (see Bibliography), Tony Bushby states that if the Vatican was serious about correcting the Vulgate, all they have to do is go downstairs into their secret Vatican archives and get the real documents. Edmond Szekely, who once had access, reported that a "beautiful copy" of Jerome's manuscripts, believed lost in the Fifth Century (and what the Vulgate should be *truly* based on), exists there.

Promises, Promises

Out of all promises made, the ones made by God should be kept. Let's take a look at Jehovah and the promises he made to his people. Everyone was undoubtedly overjoyed when Jehovah made these promises. But let's see how well he keeps these promises.

> Then said the high priest, Are these things so? And he said, Men, brethren, and fathers, hearken; The God of glory appeared unto our father Abraham, when he was in Mesopotamia, before he dwelt in Charran, And said unto him, Get thee out of thy country, and from thy kindred, and come into the land which I shall shew thee. Then came he out of the land of the Chaldeans and dwelt in Charran: and from thence, when his father was dead, he removed him into this land, wherein ye now dwell. And he gave him none inheritance in it, no, not so much as to set his foot on: yet he promised that he would give it to him for a possession, and to his seed after him, when as yet he had no child.
>
> *Acts 7:1-5*

During a fit of anger good ol' Jehovah had even announced to his people that he was breaking this promise. He said they would "know my breach of promise" because they would all die without ever seeing the Promised Land (Numbers 14:34-35). Later on he became "generous" and allowed just two people in—but all the others whom he promised never made it.

Abraham was promised a great country, including all the land between the river of Egypt and the Euphrates. Never happened. He was supposed to be the head of a great nation, but it self-destructed in the hands of Jehovah before it ever had a chance.

For those who don't think this example is clear enough, let's look at another. Here we find God promising Abraham:

> And I will give unto thee, and to thy seed after thee, the land wherein thou art a stranger, all the land of Canaan, for an everlasting possession; and I will be their God.
>
> *Genesis 17:8*

So what happened? Abraham and his "seed" got *nothing*. Zilch. The Israelites should have said, "Sure, just give us the land, *first*, pal. Then we'll think about worshipping you as a god, okay?" But this is what happened instead:

> By faith Abraham, when he was called to go out into a place which he should after receive for an inheritance, obeyed; and he went out, not knowing whither he went. By faith he sojourned in the land of promise, as in a strange country, dwelling in tabernacles with Isaac and Jacob, the heirs with him of the same promise:... also Sara herself received strength to conceive seed, and was delivered of a child... Therefore sprang there... so many as the stars of the sky in multitude... These all died in faith, not having received the promises, but having seen them afar off...
>
> *Hebrews 11:8–13*

This god could not be trusted. He could not be trusted to treat his people in a decent and kindly manner, and could not be trusted to live up to any promises that he made to them. In Numbers 10:9 he promised them that he would deliver them from their enemies whenever they were hard pressed:

> And if ye go to war in your land against the enemy that oppresseth you, then ye shall blow an alarm with the trumpets; and ye shall be remembered before the Lord your God, and ye shall be saved from your enemies.

In other words, Jehovah was saying, "Just blow this trumpet whenever you're in trouble, and I'll come down and stomp on anybody that's invading your land." Sounds great. A sacred promise of protection! Unfortunately, it wasn't kept. In the history of the world, no nation has been as abused as Israel. They have been the slaves of Babylonians, Assyrians, Turks, Greeks, Philistines, Persians, and the Syrians, among others. Where was Jehovah when all this happened? I thought they were supposed to just blow a trumpet, and old Jehovah would come running. He was always so anxious to inflict punishment that it seems he would relish the opportunity to rush in and protect his faithful followers. So what happened? Apparently, each time the trumpets would blow, Jehovah was busy with some other important task like throwing rocks or sleeping (see Nah. 1:6 or Psalms 44:23). Of course in earlier days he always made time to severely punish his *own* people for all kinds of inane reasons. These punishments occurred years before the invading tribes came in, so it seems Jehovah just got tired of punishing, killing, and enslaving his followers, so sent in other nations to do it for him later on.

Another important point to bring out is the consistent mistreatment of women and children by Jehovah. Many slaughters were ordered that included the deaths of innocent women and children. Today, numerous people in the women's rights movement convincingly contend that the Bible is a primary cause for the mistreatment of women because it has promoted it from the very beginning. Women have been forced into a subservient role by the sheer dominance and forcefulness of Jehovah and his bullying influence when, in earlier times, it was the goddess that was respected and revered. Countless examples exist of the degradation of women in the Bible. Just one that comes to mind is that women were considered unclean beings. In the 12th chapter of Leviticus it is stated that when a woman mothered a boy, she could not enter the sanctuary for 40 days. If she mothered a girl the time was doubled to 80 days, making it twice as sinful and unclean to bear a female than a male. It is also said in the same chapter that a woman is unclean for 7 days if bearing a boy, but for 14 days in the case of a girl.

As humans, we consider it the epitome of love and sweetness to see a mother holding dearly her newborn babe. But in this case it is sinful, and when the Jews were in the desert all mothers were commanded to bring a sin offering of two doves to the priests for having had children. It was law. Women were the unclean ones, the sinners, for bringing forth the miracle of life. We've been trying to correct this mistaken view and its resulting reverberations for centuries.

SEVEN

HOW TO EXPOSE A FALSE GOD

*We need to free ourselves from the
idea of God's law as a statute
imposed on us from without and to
substitute that of his spirit as a prin -
ciple governing life from within.*

—William Adams Brown

*What really interests me is whether
God had any choice in the creation of
the world.*

—Albert Einstein

Wisdom: should that not be the most important attribute of anyone's God? I would think so. But did Jehovah always display great wisdom? It is hard to find a time when he displayed *any* wisdom. When Korah, Abiram, and Dathan planned a rebellion against Moses, Jehovah became angry and caused the earth to open up and swallow all the guilty ones and their families. Fine. Not exactly a display of wisdom here—but then Jehovah *totally* loses his mind and sends down an additional fire that kills 250 more people who were guilty of nothing more than having listened to the guilty ones (sympathizers, if you will). Was this displaying the wisdom of a compassionate God?

Jehovah had a real problem with his temper. He was always "losing it," and the Bible speaks of "the anger of the Lord" continually. One of the Psalmists stated that Jehovah was angry every day. This seems to have been a natural state for him. Yet. . .

Be not hasty in thy spirit to be angry:
for anger resteth in the bosom of
fools.

Ecclesiastes 7:9

A great truism for mankind, with far reaching implications. If anger is wrong for a man, is it right for a God? NO! (I say angrily) NO! It is the God who should set the example! Otherwise, he is not worthy of being worshipped. A God without a sense of ethics is nothing but an imposter.

The Fear Factor

Here is another example of the lack of ethics with Jehovah. When he commands Abraham to take his son Isaac and sacrifice

Jehovah has Korah, Dathan, and Abiram swallowed up by the Earth

him as a burnt offering, Abraham takes the command very seriously. He had waited one hundred years to sire this son, but is now commanded by God to slay him. They travel for days to reach the appointed spot, chosen by Jehovah, while Isaac gradually learns of his father's plans.

Abraham has no idea that this is a test, and clearly goes through tremendous heartache and anguish over what he must do. Upon the mountain, Abraham readies his blade and is about to kill his son—who is by this time terrified out of his mind. At the last moment, Jehovah intervenes and stops the murder.

Why does he put an old man through such a terrible test? And why does he allow such trauma to be inflicted on a young man who will never fully recover? Jehovah provides the answer by stating,

> Lay not thine hand upon the lad, nei-
> ther do thou anything unto him: for
> now I know that thou fearest God,
> seeing thou hast not withheld thy son,
> thine only son from me.

Genesis 22:12

So Jehovah's motivation is made clear—he was trying to discover if Abraham feared him. The answer was "yes," Abraham feared his god so much, that he would kill his own son. Is this a moral act of "God?" To strike fear into the hearts of his people—to test them through murderous "set-ups?" This kind of thing tells people that fearing God is a virtue; that if you fear God everything will be okay.

I propose that there is a True God in existence who is an all-loving God. There is no need to fear Him. But this God is not Jehovah. Jehovah is an imposter. Jehovah is a pretender-god who was in charge of a small tribal following. The True God of this entire world and universe would represent us *all,* universally, as one entire family of sentient beings. He would not take "chosen ones" over all others, treat them badly, murder many of them, and goad them into attacking and killing off other tribes who happened to worship other Gods.

> He said, "I am a jealous God, and
> there is no other God beside me." But
> by announcing this he indicated to the
> angels . . . that another God does
> exist; for if there were no other one,
> of whom would he be jealous?

The Secret Book of John

Lot and his "righteous" daughters – a very close family!

Yes, Jehovah was a jealous god—who admitted his jealousy openly. The True God is far above jealousy. The True God would not harm or kill His followers and the True God would never allow His people to harm or kill other people, physically or psychologically. These things are evil—and the True God, the "God Beyond god," as Paul Tillich calls Him, is not an evil God.

Let us bring forth one more example of the moral fabric of Jehovah. Let's use Sodom and Gomorrah. Jehovah says he will destroy both cities unless ten righteous inhabitants are found. Lot, who lives in Sodom and is Abraham's nephew, is deemed righteous along with his three family members. That leaves them six short of a righteous bunch, so Jehovah destroys both cities. While the fire and brimstone was raining down, these righteous ones left the city safely—but a short distance away, Lot's wife turned back toward the destruction and was transformed into a "pillar of salt." So only three righteous ones remained—Lot and his two daughters, deemed righteous by the Lord.

Keep in mind what happens next and remember, only two cities were destroyed here—Sodom and Gomorrah—not the entire world. We find Lot fearful of living in Zoar, a neighboring town, so he dwells in a cave with his daughters.

> And the firstborn said unto the younger, Our father is old and there is not a man in the earth to come in unto us after the manner of all the earth: Come let us make our father drink wine, and we will lie with him, that we may preserve seed of our father. And they made their father drink wine that night: and the firstborn went in, and lay with her father; and he perceived not when she lay down, nor when she arose. And it came to pass on the morrow, that the firstborn said unto the younger, Behold, I lay yesternight with my father: let us make him drink wine this night also; and go thou in, and lie with him, that we may preserve seed of our father. And they made their father drink wine that night also: and the younger arose, and lay with him; and he perceived not when she lay down, nor

> when she arose. Thus were both the
> daughters of Lot with child by their
> father.

Genesis 19:31–36

These are the three who were spared by Jehovah because they were the only "righteous" ones. I am convinced that the True God can look into the hearts of people and know them to be good and righteous people instead of finding out the hard way, later. Jehovah is clearly not the True God.

The True God would not have destroyed Sodom and Gomorrah. He would have used His compassion and wisdom to teach His children proper conduct, should he desire to change them, rather than impatiently murdering them all. Jehovah was sick. He was demented.

Sure, there was a problem in these cities. It was homosexuality. Jehovah felt that homosexuality was very evil. That might be the case, depending on your own ethics and upbringing, but we are not here to judge whether it is or not. The point is, Jehovah believed it to be terribly evil. What does he ultimately do? He wipes out the cities. Jehovah punished Adam and Eve for knowing good from evil, then punished the people of Sodom and Gomorrah for *not* knowing good from evil. You can't win with this guy. He will always find a way to punish you.

Let's get back to the last Bible quote in Genesis 19. Please read it again if you need to. In effect, Jehovah is saying, "I will kill you for homosexuality, but incest is okay." He does nothing to punish Lot or his daughters for incest because they were "righteous."

The daughters clearly knew that their father had been afraid to live in Zoar, another city (probably thinking that that one would be destroyed next). So why does the Bible have the daughters say there are no other men on the earth? Jehovah's previous edict was against Sodom and Gomorrah only, and no others. Lot warns his daughter's husbands in Genesis 19:14 that "this city" (not the world) will be destroyed by the Lord. They were warned to leave the city so they would be *safe elsewhere*. So why do the women use the excuse of there being no other men upon the earth? So they can fornicate with their father?

The flimsy excuse of no other men on earth, undoubtedly made by Bible editors, does not hold up. These women planned and then engaged in incest with their own father, a vile, evil deed according to the Bible, and knew exactly what they were doing. The all knowing Jehovah, consumed with his hatred for homosexuals, just stood by and let it happen. These gals were righteous, you know.

Thou Shalt Go Ahead and Steal

The Ten Commandments are said to come from Jehovah. One of them states, "Thou shalt not steal." Seems pretty basic. So what explains this passage?

> And I will give this people favour in the sight of the Egyptians: and it shall come to pass, that, when ye go, ye shall not go empty: But every woman shall borrow of her neighbor, and of her that sojourneth in her house, jewels of silver, and jewels of gold, and raiment: and ye shall put them upon your sons, and upon your daughters; and ye shall spoil the Egyptians.
>
> *Exodus 3:21-22* (see also *Exodus 12:35–36*)

Look up the word "spoil" in any dictionary. It means "to plunder, or to steal." So Jehovah is telling his people to steal. The complete reversal of his "commandment." So what's new with this mentally deranged entity? "Thou shalt steal." If we go ahead and follow this example, killing would be okay, too, with all the murders he committed. And lying (for instance, to Adam and Eve). What else is left that falls into the category of downright rotten and criminal behavior? It never ends with this guy.

So who are you praying to these days? Is it God or the devil? Be sure you know the difference before you start asking for favors.

Compassion: A Key Component

Does Jehovah, as God, really care about you? Let's see. In the Old Testament Jehovah gives his people nothing to hope for beyond this life. Absolutely no concept of heaven or an afterlife "reward" exists in any spiritual sense. If he *is* God, could he not offer some hope or reward? His people are merely there to serve him in all of his bizarre, manipulative, and often warped ways. But Jehovah would have the power to reward his people if he so chose. We find this in Job 11:8-9, where it says that his power to do and know things is as high as heaven, with the measure thereof "longer than the earth, and broader than the sea." But does he ever use this power to do anything besides punish and torment his people? Not too often, and never in a spiritually meaningful way.

If Jehovah loved all people, why are there so many terrible injustices in the world? Remember, there is no devil for the Israelites. So why are good and bad people alike hit haphazardly

isease, famine, floods, and other disasters? Why did Jehovah
: insects and fierce animals to harass his people, whom he
osedly loved?

Does a God love his people in such a way that he comes down
and teaches them how to make bread with their own excrement?

> And thou shalt eat it as barley cakes,
> and thou shalt bake it with dung that
> cometh out of man, in their sight. And
> the Lord said, "Even thus shall the
> children of Israel eat their defiled
> bread. . ."
>
> *Ezekiel 4:12-13*

Is this what the "chosen people" were chosen for?

Jehovah stated in the Bible (Ex. 20:5) that he would put his
anger upon the following four generations of those who hated him,
and for those who loved him he would have mercy for *that* generation only. Simple math proves that Jehovah's hatred was four
times greater than his love! Any first grader could figure that out.

This interesting point, just stated, was brought to my attention
by Dr. Carroll Bierbower, a minister and researcher who sees the
Bible and what it really says quite clearly.

He also pointed out the following: How can Christians gen-
uinely accept Jehovah as God with all the evil things he had done?
It's because many believe he had later changed into a loving God.
But Jehovah himself said he never changed, not ever, and was not
a changeable God. Any good and decent Christian should have a
problem with this. If Christ came for anything, he came to free us
from this tyranny that had been imposed on us—not to support it.

For example, at one point Moses goes to Jehovah and com-
plains of having a speech impediment. Jehovah then boasts that he
is the cause of not only Moses' problem, but some pretty awful
afflictions on the human race.

> Who hath made man's mouth? Or
> who maketh the dumb, or deaf, or the
> seeing, or the blind? Have not I, the
> Lord?
>
> *Exodus 4:11*

The answer is obvious. There's no devil to pin the blame on—
he wasn't invented yet (by the Church). Jehovah gladly took credit for making people blind, deaf, and dumb. He seems to be saying
to Moses, "So, you have a speech impediment, do you? That's too

bad. But that's *nothing* compared to all the people I've afflicted who can't even talk or hear or speak. So consider yourself lucky."

The Old Testament states there is no such thing as reincarnation. So, according to Jehovah, people have nothing to look forward to after life, as well as during it.

> So a man lieth down, and riseth not:
> till the heavens be no more, they shall
> not awake, nor be raised out of their
> sleep.

Job 14:12

This means there is also no karma (past actions from one life affecting another one). So what is the purpose of people enduring such pain and hardship? Notice how Jehovah never gives a reason as to why he has put his people through so much suffering. Has it begun to dawn on you that Jehovah was not a really fun guy?

There *is* a God who is fun. He is fair, He is just, He is compassionate. He exists. He is not a man, or in the form of a man, with a long beard and flowing robes. This god in human form does not exist. The True God that exists is a force. Experiencing love provides us with a genuine taste of this force—but compared to the True God, it is only the tiny droplet from a large ocean, or the wafting of a slight summer breeze, barely discernable, as opposed to a gale-force hurricane.

Yet, the True God is not destructive. All things destructive are set apart from the True God. This means the entire earth is set apart from the True God.

Something has delivered us away from God and placed a wedge between us and our True Home. The Apostle Paul stated in his Galatian letter, "O foolish Galatians, who has bewitched you that you should not obey the truth?" He is associating the influence of Jehovah here with witchcraft and a false belief system. We are being manipulated and deceived, and Jehovah played (and may still be playing) a crucial role in this deception.

The true God loves His creations unconditionally. He forgives sinners because of that love as long as they acknowledge the wrongdoing and repent. This is the God that Jesus talks about. Judeo-Christianity, on the other hand, teaches that God does not forgive sinners because of His love, but because His wrath was appeased by the bloody sacrifice of a pure and innocent person (Jesus). This now satisfies God's sense of "justice" and causes people to be "saved," should they believe it. The idea of the sacrifice of a saviour, however, is originally pagan and not based on

Christianity at all. For example, the book *The World's Sixteen Crucified Saviors*, by Kersey Graves outlines how fifteen previous religions to Christianity had a savior who was born of a virgin, died for their sins, rose from the dead, and shares other similar points to the Christian story. None of this is new. However, what is new, from strictly the Christian standpoint, is the loving God introduced by Jesus. It was Marcion who first made this distinction sometime around 140 AD, separating an inferior creator God, whom he considered evil, from a higher One. Marcion was a Christian who insisted that Jesus came to free us from the vengeful Hebrew God and bring us into the realm of his loving Father. He proposed a canon separate from the Old Testament, but his ideas were suppressed and eventually stamped out as heresy. To this day the Old and New Testaments are "married" together, yet present two separate Gods. That's why they call it "Judeo-Christianity." This is only part of the overall spiritual deception that is being perpetrated on us all.

Various hateful things orchestrated or performed by Jehovah have been brought out in this work. The True God is, however, nothing but love. Absolutely nowhere in the Bible does it say that the True God (our Heavenly Father) punishes anyone, hates anyone, or is worshipped out of fear. Jesus said to love our enemies while Jehovah told the Israelites to hate them. It seems that, to this day, people are more intent on hatred.

One should never give up hope, even with all the misery and terrible things occurring in the world. There is still joy. We can experience it in a constant state, but never on this earth. On this earth, we can have only fleeting glimpses.

Some people have become "enlightened," so to speak. They see beyond the veil, and their "glimpses" have grown into longer looks. They have *experienced* God. You can, too. But you will never experience God by being *told* what to believe. You must make an effort to *experience*, rather than *believe*. That is where religion has gone wrong.

By experience, I do not mean experiencing God by having Jehovah come down and beat the crap out of you. It is an inner experience I am referring to. Fear plays no part in God, the True God.

There was a conversation Jesus had with a woman at the well. He told her, "neither in this mountain nor in Jerusalem do they worship the Father." They were worshipping Jehovah, and not the True God.

Jesus taught the twelve apostles to pray to "our Father who art in Heaven," changing them over from the influence of Jehovah (they were all raised to pray to Jehovah). Jesus would never have made this change with his apostles if Jehovah and the Heavenly Father were one and the same.

The early Gnostics took things a step further. The word "gnosis," in Greek, means "to know." They were considered heretics by the Christian church. The gnostics believed in experiencing the True God instead of being told what to believe by the Church. They were mystics, and many were successful in their endeavors. We are all unique individuals, all with a different path to God. No one else can be on the exact same spiritual path as you are because each of us have our own lessons to learn. By exploring what these lessons are deeply, and in our own way, we can experience God. It is an individual quest, and a powerful experience once achieved. I recall a quote, forgetting who said it, but it states, "Religion is for the masses; spirituality is for the individual."

The Church, however, did not like the idea of people "doing their own thing" because what they had in mind was *organized religion*. In other words, to control the masses in an organized way and make a business out of it. In order to make things "organized," the Church had to simplify some complex truths, and get rid of many others completely. This way, the masses are controlled. They don't have to think much, but just accept and believe. When people came to the church for salvation they were also at their mercy economically, more so than today. The church has grown into a huge business, run mainly by the Vatican, controlling large numbers of people and money is involved.

In controlling large numbers of people, the truth gets lost or diluted. It is a simple, necessary rule. Even before churches were developed Jehovah appeared and wasted no time in destroying valuable truths and replacing them with terror, in order to control. To this day, we are still attempting to recover.

Attila Szoradi, author of the manuscript *God or Satan?*, mentioned that if you take the letters of Jehovah's statement, "I am God," and shuffle them slightly, you come up with something completely different. "I go mad." Maybe he was dyslexic and got the letters mixed up. When it became "I am God," he believed it! Regardless, as this book attests, Jehovah was indeed, totally mad.

The purpose of this work has been to point out the terrible deeds of Jehovah, in hopes of bringing some sanity back into the world. I hope you have become more sane by reading this.

**Moses with The Ten Commandments: Laws so
powerful that Jehovah himself could not follow them!**

APPENDIX

BIBLICAL REFERENCES TO JEHOVAH
Or
ALL THE DIRT ON JEHOVAH, SOURCED DIRECTLY FROM HIS OWN "HOLY BOOK"

What follows is a list of Biblical references that reveal who and what Jehovah was, and exactly what he did to his followers and others. It is a list of lies, atrocities, and murders and, believe it or not, is by no means complete. Anyone checking this list and reading the Bible passages could not possibly come away with the idea that Jehovah/Yahweh was or is the true God, or a God of love. It would make no sense.

In previous editions we extended an open challenge for anyone to compile and send in a list of wonderful things Jehovah did, to be included in this edition (we were willing to spare a few lines). Such a list would exist, but we had no takers. It would be slightly larger if it included times Jehovah decided NOT to kill people at the last minute, which was mighty big of him.

> Key: To find the Bible chapter needed when numbers alone are encountered, one must simply back track to the last chapter name that was referenced.

ACTIONS OF JEHOVAH, PHYSICALLY DONE

awakes (Ps. 78:65), bends bow (Lam. 2:4), blows trumpet (Zech. 9:14), breathes (2 Sam. 22:16), builds a house (Ps. 127:1), makes and engraves tables (Ex. 32:16), cries (Is. 42:14), flew (2 Sam. 22:11), hears (Micah 7:7), laughs (Ps. 37:13), makes coats (Gen. 3:21), rides horses (Hab. 3:8), rises (Job 31:14), sees (Gen. 16:13), to shoot (Ps. 64:7), sleeps (Ps. 44:23), smells (Gen. 8:21), stands (Acts 23:11), talks (Deut. 5:24), throws rocks (Nah. 1:6), tires (Is. 1:14), touches (Job 19:21), walks (Lev. 26:12), to whet a sword (Ps. 7:12), writes (Ex. 31:18).

ANATOMY OF JEHOVAH

arms (Ps. 89:13), a bosom (Ps. 74:11), eyes (2 Chr. 16:9), a face (Ex. 33:20), ears (I Pet. 3:12), feet (Ps. 18:9), hair (Dan. 7:9), a finger (Ex. 31:18), back parts (Ex. 33:23), bowels (Jer. 31:20), a head (Dan 7:9), shoulders (Deut. 33:12), lips (Isa. 30:27), nostrils (2 Sam. 22:9), and a tongue (Isa. 30:27).

APPEARANCES OF JEHOVAH IN PHYSICAL FORM

Gen. 11:5, 17:1, 17:22, 18:1, 18:21-23, 26:2, 26:24, 35:7-14. In Ex. 19:11 he was "in sight of all the people," in Ex. 24:9-11 seventy-four people saw God, and in Ex. 33:9-11 he was seen "face to face." There is also Num. 12:3-5, Deut. 5:4, 5:24, 34:10, 1 Sam. 3:21, 2 Chr. 18:18, Job 42:5, Ezek. 1:28, and Acts 23:11.

BELLIGERENCE AND RUTHLESSNESS OF JEHOVAH

Gen. 35:5; Ex. 14:14, 14:25-28, 15:3 and 17:16; Deut. 4:33-35, 7:21-24, 10:17-21, 11:25, 20:1-4, 20:16-17, 31:3, 32:21-26 and 32:39-42; Josh. 5:13-14, 10:25; 1 Sam. 2:25, 17:45-47; 2 Sam. 22:35; 2 Chr. 20:15-17; Neh 4:20; Psalms 18:34-40, 24:8 and 144:1; Isaiah 13:4, 31:4, 42:13 and 66:15-17; Jer. 1:19, 21:5-12, 48:10, 50:25 and 51:11; Joel 2:10-11 and 3:10; Zech. 8:10, 9:14-16 and 14:3; 2 Cor. 5:11; and Heb. 10:31.

CANNIBALISM — THREATENED, PREDICTED, OR CARRIED OUT BY JEHOVAH

Lev. 26:29; 2 Kings 6:27; Is. 49:26; Jer. 19:9; Lam. 2:20; Lam. 4:10; and Ezek. 5:10.

COMMANDMENTS GIVEN, WITH EXTREME PUNISHMENT FOR BREAKING

Ex. 31:14-15; Lev. 20:10-21, 21:9 and 24:10-16; Num. 5:12-27, 15:32-36; Deut 13:6-10, 13:12-16, 17:2-6, 21:18-21, 22:21; and Zech. 13:3.

DECEPTION BY JEHOVAH

1 Kings 22:23; 2 Chr. 18-22; Is. 19:14, 66:4; Jer. 4:10, 18:11, 20:7 and 51:11; Ezek. 14:9 and 20:25-26.

DISHONESTY — CHEATING, STEALING, AND MORE, OFTEN AT JEHOVAH'S ORDERS

Gen 17:8, 25:29-34, 27:6-26, 30:37-43 and 34:6-31; Ex. 3:18-22; Deut. 3:7, 14:21 and 20:10-15; Josh. 24:13; Jud. 11:21-24; 1 Kings 22:20-23; 2 Kings 8:10; 1 Chr. 5:21, 26:27; and 2 Chr. 20:25.

EVIL CARRIED OUT OR THREATENED BY JEHOVAH

Jud. 2:15, 9:23; 1 Sam. 16:14-15, 18:10; 2 Sam. 21:11, 24:15-16; 1 Kings 14:10, 22:23; 2 Kings 21:12-15; 2 Chr. 18:22; Isa. 19:14, 31:2 and 45:7; Jer. 1:14-16, 11:11, 11:17, 11:23, 18:7, 18:11, 19:15, 21:9-12, 25:29, 32:42, 35:17, 36:3, 44:2, 44:11, 44:27-29, 45:5; and Amos 3:6.

HOSTILITY OF JEHOVAH

Ps. 2:12, 6:1, 7:6, 7:11, 21:9, 27:9, 38:3, 47:2, 56:7, 59:13, 68:35, 69:24, 74:1-2, 76:12, 77:9, 78:21, 78:31, 78:49-50, 78:58-66, 79:5, 80:4-6, 106:29, 106:32 and 106:40.

INFANTS OR CHILDREN KILLED, SUGGESTED OR CARRIED OUT BY JEHOVAH

Lev. 26:22; Num. 31:17; Deut 3:6; 1 Sam. 15:3; 2 Sam. 12:15-18; Ps. 137:8-9; Isa. 14:21, 13:18; Jer. 2:30, 15:7 and 18:21; Lam. 4:10; Ezek. 9:6; Hos. 2:4, 9:12 and 13:16.

INNOCENT PEOPLE PUNISHED BY JEHOVAH

Gen. 9:20-25, 20:18; Ex. 12:29-30, 20:5; Lev. 21:17-21; Deut. 5:9; 1 Sam. 3:11-14; 2 Sam. 5:8; Job 1:1-19, 2:1-7, 30:20-31; and Isa. 14:21.

JEALOUSY OF JEHOVAH

Ex. 20:5, 34:14; Deut 4:24, 5:9, 6:14-15 and 29:20; Ps. 79:5; Ezek. 16:38, 36:5-6 and 38:19; Nah. 1:2; Hab. 3:8; and Zech. 8:2.

KILLINGS BY JEHOVAH, WITH HIS HELP OR UNDER HIS COMMAND

Gen. 5:24, 7:21-23, 19:24-25, 38:7 and 38:10, Ex. 12:29-30, 32:25-28 (3,000 killed); Lev. 10:1-2; Num. 11:1 (many burned to death by Jehovah), 14:26-37, 16:32-35, 16:44-49 (14,700 killed), 21:5-6, 25:1-9 (24,000 killed), 31:7-18 and 33:4; Deut. 2:20-21, 2:30-34 and 3:3-7 (people of 60 cities and other towns); Josh. 6:21-24, 8:25-28 (12,000 killed), 10:10-13, 10:28-42 and 11:6-14; Jud. 1:4 (10,000 killed), 3:29 (10,000 killed), 8:10 (120,000 killed), 11:32-33, 12:6 (42,000 killed), 18:27, 20:23-25 (18,000 killed), 20:35 (25,000 killed) and 20:48; 1 Sam. 6:19 (Jehovah kills 50,070), 15:1-8 (all Amalekites), 23:1-5, 25:39 (Jehovah murders Nabal), 27:7-11 (all Amalekites again), 30:1-2 and 30:8 & 30:17 (all Amalekites except for 400); 2 Sam. 5:19-25, 6:6-7 (Uzzah killed by Jehovah for steadying the ark), 8:1-5, 8:13 (18,000 killed), 10:18 (more than 40,000 killed), 12:14-18 (David's infant child murdered by Jehovah), 23:10-12 and 24:15 (70,000 killed); 1 Kings 18:19&40 (450 prophets killed), 20:28-30 (100,000 killed); 2 Kings 1:10-12, 2:23-24 (42 children killed), 10:17-30, 17:25 (lions sent by Jehovah to kill people) and 19:35 (angel of the Lord kills 185,000); 1 Chr. 5:19-22, 10:13-14 (the Lord kills King Saul); 2 Chr. 13:15-18 (500,000 killed), 13:20 (the Lord murders Jeroboam), 14:8-15 (one *million* killed), 20:22-25, 25:11-12 (10,000 killed twice = 20,000 dead), 28:5-8 (120,000 killed) and 36:15-17; Esther 9:9-13 (510 killed); Jer. 33:5; Lam. 2:1-22, 5:43; Ezek. 9:5-10.

LACK OF OMNIPOTENCE BY JEHOVAH

Ex. 4:24; Jud. 1:19 and Jer. 2:30.

LACK OF OMNIPRESENCE BY JEHOVAH

Gen. 4:16, 11:5, 17:22, 18:20-21 and 18:33; Ex. 11:4, 20:24, 25:8 and 29:43-46; Num. 23:15; Deut 23:13-14, 33:2; 2 Sam 7:5-7; 1 Kings 8:12-13, 19:11-12; 2 Kings 24:20; Job 1:12, 2:7; Ps. 9:11, 10:1, 14:1-2, 22:1, 74:2 and 76:2; Is. 24:23, 37:14; Jer. 23:39-40; Ezek. 20:40; Hos 11:9, 12:9; Joel 3:17; Jonah 1:3, 1:10; Hab 3:3, Zech. 8:2-3.

LACK OF OMNISCIENCE (ALL KNOWING) BY JEHOVAH

Gen. 11:1-8, 18:20-1 and 22:12; Num. 22:9; Deut. 8:2, 13:3; 2 Chr. 32:31; Jer. 32:35, 36:3&7; Amos 3:2.

MERCILESSNESS OF JEHOVAH

Deut. 7:2, 7:16 and 20:12-17; Ps. 1:4-9; Isa. 9:17-20; Jer. 20:16.

PLAGUES AND AFFLICTIONS SENT BY JEHOVAH ON HUMANS (Plagues on animals are not included here, unless they happened to coincidentally experience the same human problem.)

Ex. 8:6-7, 8:16-17, 9:8-10, 9:22-25 and 10:12-15; Num. 16:44-49 (plague kills 14,700), 25:1-9 (plague kills 24,000); 1 Sam. 5:6-12; 2 Sam. 24:15 (70,000 killed); 2 Kings 5:25-27, 6:15-18 (blinds people), 15:1-5; 2 Chr. 26:19-20; Ps. 44:9-24; Lam. 1:12; Micah 4:6; Nah 1:12.

PROMISES BROKEN BY JEHOVAH

Num. 10:9, which was clearly broken (see supporting text), 14:34, 26:65 (confirms this breach—only two Israelites entered the Promised Land). See also Acts 7:1-5.

REPENTENCE BY JEHOVAH — PROMISED OR ACCOMPLISHED

Jehovah repented so much that, according to Jer. 15:6, he once got tired of doing it.

Gen. 6:6-7; Ex. 32:14; Jud. 2:18; 1 Sam. 15:10, 15:11 and 15:35; 2 Sam. 24:15-16; Ps. 106:45; Jer. 18:8, 26:3, 26:19 and 42:10; Joel 2:13; Amos 7:3, 7:6; Jonah 3:10.

REPRIMAND OF JEHOVAH

Ex. 5:22, 32:9-14 (Moses wins an argument with Jehovah and causes him to repent); Num. 11:10-15, 14:11-20 (Moses convinces Jehovah to change his mind); Josh. 7:6-9; 2 Sam. 24:17 (David reprimands Jehovah for slaughtering people); Ps. 82:2; Jer. 15:18; Lam. 1:12; Ezek. 9:6; Zech. 1:12.

SLAVERY ORDERED, UPHELD, OR PRACTICED PER JEHOVAH

Deut. 20:10-11 (enslavement ordered on large scale); Ex. 21:1-7, 21:20-21; Deut. 15:12, 15:16 and 15:17; 2 Chr. 12:5-8.

TEMPTATION BY JEHOVAH (rather than the devil)

Gen. 22:1-3 (tempts Abraham); Deut. 4:34.

THREATS BY JEHOVAH

A list of diabolical threats in case his orders were not obeyed. Many times it is not known if such threats were carried out when the orders were ignored, but we are at least certain of the verbal abuse.

To kill followers, (Ex. 22:24); Lev. 26:16-33; Deut. 28:15-68, 31:15-21; 1 Kings 14:10-15, 16:1-4; Isa. 9:17-20, 13:6-22, 19:1-5 and 35:1-5; Jer. 4:26-28, 6:11-13, 7:20, 7:30-34, 8:10, 9:11-22, 11:22-23, 13:12-14, 15:1-7, 15:14, 16:1-9, 19:7-11, 23:39-40, 24:9-10, 25:9-38, 27:8, 29:17-18, 32:36, 34:20-22, 38:2, 42:17-22, 44:11-13, 48:7-10, 49:2, 49:13, 49:17, 49:33-37, 51:29-40 and 51:57; Ezek. 5:12-17, 6:5-14, 7:1-9, 8:18, 13:13, 21:1-5, 21:31-32, 25:13-14, 26:3-21, 29:3, 29:8&11, 30:5&15, 31:18, 32:15, 32:30-32, 34:16, 38:18-23, 39:3-5 and 39:17-19; Hos. 13:7-16; Amos 1:4-14, 2:1-5, 6:8, 8:9-14 and 9:1-3; Zeph. 1:1-5, 3:8; Zech. 14:12; Mal. 2:3, 4:5-6. This last entry in Malachi reflects what is said at the end of the Old Testament—with Jehovah talking about "the coming of the great and dreadful day of the Lord," including his paradoxical action of taking steps to protect mankind against *him - self* (Jehovah), "lest I come and smite the earth with a curse."

VAINGLORIOUSNESS (EXCESSIVE POWER OR VANITY) OF JEHOVAH

Gen. 22:9-12 (forces Abraham to almost murder his son, Isaac, just to see if Abraham fears him), Ex. 9:15-16 (kills people with pestilence just to show his power), 10:1-2; Jud. 7:2; Ezek. 6:14.

VINDICTIVENESS OF JEHOVAH

Num. 11:31-34; Ps. 94:1; Isa. 34:1-15; Jer. 5:29-31, 9:9, 46:10, 50:13-15 and 51:36; Rom. 12:19; Heb. 10:30-31.

WOMEN DISCRIMINATED AGAINST, USUALLY PER JOHAVAH OR HIS LAWS

Gen. 3:16; Lev. 12:1-9, 15:16-33; Num. 5:12-27, 31:7-18; Deut. 21:10-13, 24:1-2; Jud. 5:30-31, 19:24-25 and 21:10-23; 2 Kings 15:16; Esther 2:2, 2:12-14; Eccl. 7:26-28; Hos. 13:16.

BIBLIOGRAPHY

4000 Errors and Unfavorable Biblical Verses, Compiled by Olin Miller, Superior Books, San Diego, CA, 1954.

The Crucifixion of Truth: The Discovery of Hidden Vatican Scrolls and the Falsehoods They Reveal About Christianity, Tony Bushby, Joshua Books, Maroochydore, Queensland, Australia, www.joshuabooks.com.

The Genius of the Few: The Story of Those Who Founded the Garden in Eden, Christian O'Brien with Barbara Joy O'Brien, Dianthus Publishing Limited, Cirencester, England, www.goldenageproject.org.uk, revised edition, 1999.

God 2000: Religion without the Bible, Dr. Paul Winchell, April Enterprises, Inc., Santa Monica, CA, 1982.

The Gods of Eden, William Bramley, Dahlin Family Press, San Jose, CA, 1989.

Holey Bible: Old Testament, J. B. McPherson, Splendor Publishing, Danville, Kentucky, 1991.

Interrogatories to Jehovah: Upon Various Subjects, to which Answers are Earnestly Desired, D.M. Bennett, Liberal and Scientific Publishing House, New York, NY, 1878.

More Steve Allen on the Bible, Religion, & Morality, Steve Allen, Prometheus Books, Buffalo, New York, 1993.

The Problem of Suffering and Evil, Dr. Carroll R. Bierbower, Grace Church, Cave Junction, OR, booklet, no date given.

Some Mistakes of Moses, Robert G. Ingersoll, C.P. Farrell Publishing Company, Washington, D.C., 1879.

Steve Allen on the Bible, Religion, & Morality, Steve Allen, Prometheus Books, Buffalo, New York, 1990.

Triumph of the Human Spirit: The Greatest Achievements of the Human Soul and How Its Power can Change Your Life, Paul Tice, The Book Tree, 1999.

INDEX

Abel, 45
Abel-shittim, 30
Abihu, 21
Abiram, 25-27, 81-82
African, 57
Alexandria, 55-56
Allen, Steve, 35
All-Knowing, 27
Amorites, 31, 44
Amos, 37
Anath, 10
Anu, 12
Aristarchus, 55
Ashera, 10
Assyrians, 24, 79
Astarte, 10
Baal, 10, 12, 29
Babylon, 33
Babylonia, 57
Babylonian Empire, 13
Babylonians, 79
Banish, 52
Barranger, Jack, 4
Basic Logic, 45
Bibles, 55
Biblical, 5, 9, 60, 93
Bierbower, Dr. Carroll, 88
Bigfoot, 66
Blackmail, 12-13
Bramley, William, 19
Brown, William Adams, 81
Cabelites, 11
Cain, 45
Campbell, Joseph, 5, 51
Canaan, 28-29, 31, 44, 78
Canaanites, 25, 31, 44
Carolus Linnaeus, 57
Central America, 56
Chaldeans, 78
Charran, 78
Cherubim, 12
Cherubims, 52
China, 57
Christ, 88
Christian Gnostic, 51
Christian, 37, 44, 51, 88, 90
Christianity, 55, 68, 90
Christians, 54, 60, 68, 88
Cloud, 13-14, 19, 21-22, 28
Coercion, 15
Columbus, Christopher, 55
Common Sense, 25, 33, 51, 61
Compassionate, 35, 45, 59, 76, 81, 89
Copernicus, 55
Creator, 9, 59, 61, 68, 76
Criminal Element, 40
Dark Ages, 55
Dathan, 25-27, 81-82
Dead, 17, 22, 28-29, 31, 57,

72-73, 75, 78
Death, 5, 15-16, 21-22, 29-30, 45, 52-54, 56, 68, 76
Debir, 47
Defections, 23-24
Demonic Element, 41
Deuteronomy, 30-31, 40, 44-45
Deva, 40
Disneyland, 57
Earth, 9, 14-15, 19, 26-28, 30, 49, 55-56, 60-61, 63-64, 81-82, 85-87, 89-90
Ecclesiastes, 81
Eden, 37-39, 49, 51-53, 61, 64
Eglon, 47
Egyptian, 69, 71, 75
Ehud, 67
Einstein, Albert, 29, 81
El, 10
Eleazar, 28
Elijah, 20
Elisha, 33
Enki, 12
Enlil, 12
Eratosthenes, 55-56
Euphrates, 78
Euripides, 40
Eye of Horus, 14
Ezekiel, 24, 37, 88
Father of Lies, 37, 39
Fear Factor, 81
Fohi, 57
Gabriel, 12
Galatians, 89
Galileo, 56
Garden of Eden, 37, 39, 49, 51, 53, 64
Gezer, 47
Gide, Andre, 63
Gnostic, 51, 58
Gnostics, 90
God, 4-5, 7, 9, 11-14, 16-17, 19, 21, 23-24, 27-31, 33, 35, 37, 39-41, 43-45, 48-49, 51-54, 57-61, 63-65, 67-69, 71-72, 75-76, 78-79, 81, 83, 85-91, 93
God-fearing, 5
Godly, 7, 10, 58, 64, 66-67
Gods, 9-15, 29-30, 39-40, 45, 51, 53, 57, 64, 69, 83, 91
Gomorrah, 85-86
Grecian, 55
Greed, 11
Greek, 55, 90
Greeks, 57, 79
Hab, 36
Heaven, 20, 24, 30, 68, 87,

90
Heavenly Father, 90
Hebrew, 7, 39
Hebrews, 35, 37, 39, 79
Hebron, 47
Hell, 11, 27, 29, 52, 64, 68, 73
Hindus, 57
Hitler, 30, 35, 67
Hittites, 44
Hivites, 44
Holback, 7
Holy, 10, 21, 52, 67, 93
Hosea, 43
Human Origins, 4
Human Soul, 4
Human Spirit, 4
Hus, Jon, 55
Impale, 29
Imperial Mandate, 55
India, 14
Ingersoll, Robert, 19, 52, 61
Isaac, 79, 81, 83
Isaiah, 8-9, 37, 44
Israeli, 29, 59
Israelite, 69
Jebusites, 44
Jehovah Relieved of Duties, 58
Jehovah, 5, 7-17, 19, 21-33, 35-37, 39-41, 43-45, 47-49, 51-54, 56-59, 61, 63-69, 71-83, 85-93
Jeremeelites, 11
Jeremiah, 23, 33, 37
Jerusalem, 33, 59, 90
Jewish Torah, 23, 26, 30
Joshua, 12, 29-30, 47, 52
Judah, 10-11, 49
Judean, 11
Judeo-Christian God, 58
Judeo-Christianity, 89-90
Jupiter, 57
Kenites, 10-11
Kibroth-hattaavah, 22-23
Kill, 10, 17, 25, 27-28, 31, 40-41, 44-45, 48, 54, 63-64, 67, 72-73, 75, 83, 85-86, 93
Killing, 16, 28, 45, 48-49, 71, 80, 83, 87
King David, 47
King James, 37
King Jehoiachin, 33
King Zedekiah, 33
Korah, 25-27, 81-82
Lachich, 47
Levite, 11
Levites, 11
Leviticus, 12-13, 15-16, 21-22, 80
Libnah, 47

Locusts, 72
Lord Jehovah, 41, 75
Lord of Spirits, 12
Lot, 11, 26, 84-86
Mafia-type tactics, 13
Makkedah, 47
Malachi, 33
Matthew, 53
Maxwell, Jordan, 4
Maya, 56
Mencken, Henry L., 57
Mesopotamia, 78
Middle East, 12, 65
Midianite, 29
Midianites, 29
Moab, 29
Moabites, 29
Mount Hor, 28
Mt. Sinai, 15, 22
Mumbo Jumbo, 57-58
Mythological Deities, 57
Mythology, 9
Nadab, 21
Near East, 16
Nebuchadnezzar, 33
Negeb, 7, 11
New Testament, 44, 52, 89
Numbers, 11, 21, 23, 26-27, 29, 40, 45, 48-49, 78-79, 91, 93
Old Testament Jehovah, 5, 19, 73, 87
Old Time Religion, 4
Ormuzd, 57
Osiris, 57
Pact, 19
Paine, Thomas, 35
Palestine, 7, 9-10
Passover, 67, 75-76
Paul, Apostle, 89
Peniel, 43
Pentateuch, 33, 61
Perizzites, 44
Persian, 40
Persians, 57, 79
Philistines, 79
Phineas, 29-30
Pol Pot, 35
Prague, 55
Promised Land, 29-31, 68, 78
Promises, 78
Psalmists, 81
Psalms, 8, 36, 80
Pythagoras, 55
Queen of Heaven, 24
Question of Evil, 35
Raphael, 12
Red Sea, 31
Religion, 4-5, 39, 69, 76, 90-91
Religious Beginnings, 4
Reubenite, 25
Romans, 57

Sabaoth, 12
Sabbath, 45-46
Salvation, 64, 91
Samael, 51
Samuel, 12, 37, 40-41, 47
Saul, 41
Secret Book of John, 83
Serpent, 39-40, 52-53, 56, 64, 69-70
Shaitan, 40
Shamash, 57
Shatan, 40
Shaw, George Bernard, 19
Sheol, 26
Shining Ones, 12-13
Simeonites, 10
Sodom, 85-86
Sophia, 55
Spirit, 4, 22, 37, 41, 81
St. Paul, 44
Stalin, 30, 35
Syrian, 12
Syrians, 79
Szoradi, Attila, 91
Tabernacle, 19
Tammuz, 24
Ten Commandments, 27, 44-45, 87, 92
Tent of Meeting, 22, 27, 29
Theologia Germanica, 63
Thiry, Paul Henri, 7
Thoreau, Henry David, 44
Thummim, 23
Thutmose III of Egypt, 14
Tillich, Paul, 85
Tribe, 10-11, 13, 21
Turks, 79
UFO, 19
UFOs, 4
Unholy Alliance, 49
Uriel, 12
Urim, 23
Vatican City, 58
Vatican, 58-59, 76, 91
Virgilius, 55
Williams, Tennessee, 7
Women, 24, 29, 45, 47, 54, 57, 64, 80, 86
YHWH, 7
Zeta Reticuli, 15
Zoar, 85-86

***Triumph of the Human Spirit: The Greatest Achievements of the Human Soul and How Its Power Can Change Your Life*, by Paul Tice.** A triumph of the human spirit happens when we know we are right about something, put our heart into achieving its goal, and then succeed. There is no better feeling. People throughout history have triumphed while fighting for the highest ideal of all -- spiritual truth. Tice brings you back to relive and explore history's most incredible spiritual moments, bringing you into the lives of visionaries and great leaders who were in touch with their souls and followed their hearts. They explored God in their own way, exposed corruption and false teachings, or freed themselves and others from suppression. People like Gandhi, Joan of Arc, and Dr. King expressed exactly what they believed and changed the entire course of history. They were eliminated through violence, but on a spiritual level achieved victory because of their strong moral cause. Their spirit lives on, and the world was greatly improved. Tice covers other movements and people who may have physically failed, but spiritually triumphed. This book not only documents the history of spiritual giants, it shows how you can achieve your own spiritual triumph. In today's world we are free to explore the truth without fear of being tortured or executed. As a result, the rewards are great. Various exercises will strengthen the soul and reveal its hidden power. One can discover their true spiritual source with this work and will be able to tap into it. This is the perfect book for all those who believe in spiritual freedom and have a passion for the truth. **ISBN 1-885395-57-4 · 295 pages · 6 x 9 · trade paper · illustrated · $19.95**

***That Old Time Religion: The Story of Religious Foundations*, by Jordan Maxwell and Paul Tice.** This book proves there is nothing new under the sun — including Christianity. It gives a complete rundown of the stellar, lunar, and solar evolution of our religious systems; contains new, long-awaited, exhaustive research on the gods and our beliefs; includes research by Dr. Alan A. Snow, famous Dead Sea Scrolls scholar, on astrology in the Dead Sea Scrolls. Dr. Snow has been referred to by Sydney Ohmarr as the "world's greatest authority on astrology and the Dead Sea Scrolls." Includes 3 chapters by Paul Tice, a well known Gnostic minister. This book is illustrated, organized, and very comprehensible. Educate yourself with clear documented proof, and be prepared to have your belief system shattered! **ISBN 1-58509-100-6 · 220 pages · 6 x 9 · trade paper · $19.95**

***Mysteries Explored: The Search for Human Origins, UFOs, and Religious Beginnings*, by Jack Barranger and Paul Tice.** Jack Barranger and Paul Tice are two authors who have combined forces in an overall investigation into human origins, religion, mythology, UFOs, and other unexplained phenomena. In the first chapter, "The Legacy of Zecharia Sitchin", Barranger covers the importance of Sitchin's *Earth Chronicles* books, which is creating a revolution in the way we look at our past. In "The First Dragon" chapter, Tice examines the earliest known story containing dragons, coming from Sumerian/Babylonian mythology. In "Past Shock", Barranger suggests that events which happened thousands of years ago very strongly impact humanity today. In "UFOs: From Earth or Outer Space?" Tice explores the evidence for aliens being from other earthly dimensions as opposed to having an extraterrestrial origin. "Is Religion Harmful?" looks at the origins of religion and why the entire idea may no longer be working for us, while "A Call to Heresy" shows how Jesus and the Buddha were considered heretics in their day, and how we have reached a critical point in our present spiritual development that requires another such leap. Aside from these chapters, the book also contains a number of outrageous (but discontinued) newsletters, including: Promethean Fire, Pleiadian Poop, and Intrusions. **ISBN 1-58509-101-4 · 104 pages · 6 x 9 · trade paper · $12.95**

102

Of Heaven and Earth: Essays Presented at the First Sitchin Studies Day, edited by Zecharia Sitchin. ISBN 1-885395-17-5 • 164 pages • 5 1/2 x 8 1/2 • trade paper • illustrated • $14.95

God Games: What Do You Do Forever?, by Neil Freer. ISBN 1-885395-39-6 • 312 pages • 6 x 9 • trade paper • $19.95

Space Travelers and the Genesis of the Human Form: Evidence of Intelligent Contact in the Solar System, by Joan d'Arc. ISBN 1-58509-127-8 • 208 pages • 6 x 9 • trade paper • illustrated • $18.95

Humanity's Extraterrestrial Origins: ET Influences on Humankind's Biological and Cultural Evolution, by Dr. Arthur David Horn with Lynette Mallory-Horn. ISBN 3-931652-31-9 • 373 pages • 6 x 9 • trade paper • $17.00

Past Shock: The Origin of Religion and Its Impact on the Human Soul, by Jack Barranger. ISBN 1-885395-08-6 • 126 pages • 6 x 9 • trade paper • illustrated • $12.95

Flying Serpents and Dragons: The Story of Mankind's Reptilian Past, by R.A. Boulay. ISBN 1-885395-38-8 • 276 pages • 6 x 9 • trade paper • illustrated • $19.95

Triumph of the Human Spirit: The Greatest Achievements of the Human Soul and How Its Power Can Change Your Life, by Paul Tice. ISBN 1-885395-57-4 • 295 pages • 6 x 9 • trade paper • illustrated • $19.95

Mysteries Explored: The Search for Human Origins, UFOs, and Religious Beginnings, by Jack Barranger and Paul Tice. ISBN 1-58509-101-4 • 104 pages • 6 x 9 • trade paper • $12.95

Mushrooms and Mankind: The Impact of Mushrooms on Human Consciousness and Religion, by James Arthur. ISBN 1-58509-151-0 • 180 pages • 6 x 9 • trade paper • $16.95

Vril or Vital Magnetism, with an Introduction by Paul Tice. ISBN 1-58509-030-1 • 124 pages • 5 1/2 x 8 1/2 • trade paper • $12.95

The Odic Force: Letters on Od and Magnetism, by Karl von Reichenbach. ISBN 1-58509-001-8 • 192 pages • 6 x 9 • trade paper • $15.95

The New Revelation: The Coming of a New Spiritual Paradigm, by Arthur Conan Doyle. ISBN 1-58509-220-7 • 124 pages • 6 x 9 • trade paper • $12.95

The Astral World: Its Scenes, Dwellers, and Phenomena, by Swami Panchadasi. ISBN 1-58509-071-9 • 104 pages • 6 x 9 • trade paper • $11.95

Reason and Belief: The Impact of Scientific Discovery on Religious and Spiritual Faith, by Sir Oliver Lodge. ISBN 1-58509-226-6 • 180 pages • 6 x 9 • trade paper • $17.95

William Blake: A Biography, by Basil De Selincourt. ISBN 1-58509-225-8 • 384 pages • 6 x 9 • trade paper • $28.95

The Divine Pymander: And Other Writings of Hermes Trismegistus, translated by John D. Chambers. ISBN 1-58509-046-8 • 196 pages • 6 x 9 • trade paper • $16.95

Theosophy and The Secret Doctrine, by Harriet L. Henderson. Includes *H.P. Blavatsky: An Outline of Her Life,* by Herbert Whyte, ISBN 1-58509-075-1 • 132 pages • 6 x 9 • trade paper • $13.95

The Light of Egypt, Volume One: The Science of the Soul and the Stars, by Thomas H. Burgoyne. ISBN 1-58509-051-4 • 320 pages • 6 x 9 • trade paper • illustrated • $24.95

The Light of Egypt, Volume Two: The Science of the Soul and the Stars, by Thomas H. Burgoyne. ISBN 1-58509-052-2 • 224 pages • 6 x 9 • trade paper • illustrated • $17.95

The Jumping Frog and 18 Other Stories: 19 Unforgettable Mark Twain Stories, by Mark Twain. ISBN 1-58509-200-2 • 128 pages • 6 x 9 • trade paper • $12.95

The Devil's Dictionary: A Guidebook for Cynics, by Ambrose Bierce. ISBN 1-58509-016-6 • 144 pages • 6 x 9 • trade paper • $12.95

The Smoky God: Or The Voyage to the Inner World, by Willis George Emerson. ISBN 1-58509-067-0 • 184 pages • 6 x 9 • trade paper • illustrated • $15.95

A Short History of the World, by H.G. Wells. ISBN 1-58509-211-8 • 320 pages • 6 x 9 • trade paper • $24.95

The Voyages and Discoveries of the Companions of Columbus, by Washington Irving. ISBN 1-58509-500-1 • 352 pages • 6 x 9 • hard cover • $39.95

History of Baalbek, by Michel Alouf. ISBN 1-58509-063-8 • 196 pages • 5 x 8 • trade paper • illustrated • $15.95

Ancient Egyptian Masonry: The Building Craft, by Sommers Clarke and R. Engelback. ISBN 1-58509-059-X • 350 pages • 6 x 9 • trade paper • illustrated • $26.95

That Old Time Religion: The Story of Religious Foundations, by Jordan Maxwell and Paul Tice. ISBN 1-58509-100-6 • 220 pages • 6 x 9 • trade paper • $19.95

Jumpin' Jehovah: Exposing the Atrocities of the Old Testament God, by Paul Tice. ISBN 1-58509-102-2 • 104 pages • 6 x 9 • trade paper • $12.95

The Book of Enoch: A Work of Visionary Revelation and Prophecy, Revealing Divine Secrets and Fantastic Information about Creation, Salvation, Heaven and Hell, translated by R. H. Charles. ISBN 1-58509-019-0 • 152 pages • 5 1/2 x 8 1/2 • trade paper • $13.95

The Book of Enoch: Translated from the Editor's Ethiopic Text and Edited with an Enlarged Introduction, Notes and Indexes, Together with a Reprint of the Greek Fragments, edited by R. H. Charles. ISBN 1-58509-080-8 • 448 pages • 6 x 9 • trade paper • $34.95

The Book of the Secrets of Enoch, translated from the Slavonic by W. R. Morfill. Edited, with Introduction and Notes by R. H. Charles. ISBN 1-58509-020-4 • 148 pages • 5 1/2 x 8 1/2 • trade paper • $13.95

Enuma Elish: The Seven Tablets of Creation, Volume One, by L. W. King. ISBN 1-58509-041-7 • 236 pages • 6 x 9 • trade paper • illustrated • $18.95

Enuma Elish: The Seven Tablets of Creation, Volume Two, by L. W. King. ISBN 1-58509-042-5 • 260 pages • 6 x 9 • trade paper • illustrated • $19.95

Enuma Elish, Volumes One and Two: The Seven Tablets of Creation, by L. W. King. Two volumes from above bound as one. ISBN 1-58509-043-3 • 496 pages • 6 x 9 • trade paper • illustrated • $38.90

The Archko Volume: Documents that Claim Proof to the Life, Death, and Resurrection of Christ, by Drs. McIntosh and Twyman. ISBN 1-58509-082-4 • 248 pages • 6 x 9 • trade paper • $20.95

The Lost Language of Symbolism: An Inquiry into the Origin of Certain Letters, Words, Names, Fairy-Tales, Folklore, and Mythologies, by Harold Bayley. ISBN 1-58509-070-0 • 384 pages • 6 x 9 • trade paper • $27.95

The Book of Jasher: A Suppressed Book that was Removed from the Bible, Referred to in Joshua and Second Samuel, translated by Albinus Alcuin (800 AD). ISBN 1-58509-081-6 • 304 pages • 6 x 9 • trade paper • $24.95

The Bible's Most Embarrassing Moments, with an Introduction by Paul Tice. ISBN 1-58509-025-5 • 172 pages • 5 x 8 • trade paper • $14.95

History of the Cross: The Pagan Origin and Idolatrous Adoption and Worship of the Image, by Henry Dana Ward. ISBN 1-58509-056-5 • 104 pages • 6 x 9 • trade paper • illustrated • $11.95

Was Jesus Influenced by Buddhism? A Comparative Study of the Lives and Thoughts of Gautama and Jesus, by Dwight Goddard. ISBN 1-58509-027-1 • 252 pages • 6 x 9 • trade paper • $19.95

History of the Christian Religion to the Year Two Hundred, by Charles B. Waite. ISBN 1-885395-15-9 • 556 pages. • 6 x 9 • hard cover • $25.00

Symbols, Sex, and the Stars, by Ernest Busenbark. ISBN 1-885395-19-1 • 396 pages • 5 1/2 x 8 1/2 • trade paper • $22.95

History of the First Council of Nice: A World's Christian Convention, A.D. 325, by Dean Dudley. ISBN 1-58509-023-9 • 132 pages • 5 1/2 x 8 1/2 • trade paper • $12.95

The World's Sixteen Crucified Saviors, by Kersey Graves. ISBN 1-58509-018-2 • 436 pages • 5 1/2 x 8 1/2 • trade paper • $29.95

Babylonian Influence on the Bible and Popular Beliefs: A Comparative Study of Genesis I.2, by A. Smythe Palmer. ISBN 1-58509-000-X • 124 pages • 6 x 9 • trade paper • $12.95

Biography of Satan: Exposing the Origins of the Devil, by Kersey Graves. ISBN 1-885395-11-6 • 168 pages • 5 1/2 x 8 1/2 • trade paper • $13.95

The Malleus Maleficarum: The Notorious Handbook Once Used to Condemn and Punish "Witches", by Heinrich Kramer and James Sprenger. ISBN 1-58509-098-0 • 332 pages • 6 x 9 • trade paper • $25.95

Crux Ansata: An Indictment of the Roman Catholic Church, by H. G. Wells. ISBN 1-58509-210-X • 160 pages • 6 x 9 • trade paper • $14.95

Emanuel Swedenborg: The Spiritual Columbus, by U.S.E. (William Spear). ISBN 1-58509-096-4 • 208 pages • 6 x 9 • trade paper • $17.95

Dragons and Dragon Lore, by Ernest Ingersoll. ISBN 1-58509-021-2 • 228 pages • 6 x 9 • trade paper • illustrated • $17.95

The Vision of God, by Nicholas of Cusa. ISBN 1-58509-004-2 • 160 pages • 5 x 8 • trade paper • $13.95

The Historical Jesus and the Mythical Christ: Separating Fact from Fiction, by Gerald Massey. ISBN 1-58509-073-5 • 244 pages • 6 x 9 • trade paper • $18.95

Gog and Magog: The Giants in Guildhall; Their Real and Legendary History, with an Account of Other Giants at Home and Abroad, by F.W. Fairholt. ISBN 1-58509-084-0 • 172 pages • 6 x 9 • trade paper • $16.95

The Origin and Evolution of Religion, by Albert Churchward. ISBN 1-58509-078-6 • 504 pages • 6 x 9 • trade paper • $39.95

The Origin of Biblical Traditions, by Albert T. Clay. ISBN 1-58509-065-4 • 220 pages • 5 1/2 x 8 1/2 • trade paper • $17.95

Aryan Sun Myths, by Sarah Elizabeth Titcomb, Introduction by Charles Morris. ISBN 1-58509-069-7 • 192 pages • 6 x 9 • trade paper • $15.95

The Social Record of Christianity, by Joseph McCabe. Includes *The Lies and Fallacies of the Encyclopedia Britannica*, ISBN 1-58509-215-0 • 204 pages • 6 x 9 • trade paper • $17.95

The History of the Christian Religion and Church During the First Three Centuries, by Dr. Augustus Neander. ISBN 1-58509-077-8 • 112 pages • 6 x 9 • trade paper • $12.95

Ancient Symbol Worship: Influence of the Phallic Idea in the Religions of Antiquity, by Hodder M. Westropp and C. Staniland Wake. ISBN 1-58509-048-4 • 120 pages • 6 x 9 • trade paper • illustrated • $12.95

The Gnosis: Or Ancient Wisdom in the Christian Scriptures, by William Kingsland. ISBN 1-58509-047-6 • 232 pages • 6 x 9 • trade paper • $18.95

The Evolution of the Idea of God: An Inquiry into the Origin of Religions, by Grant Allen. ISBN 1-58509-074-3 • 160 pages • 6 x 9 • trade paper • $14.95

Sun Lore of All Ages: A Survey of Solar Mythology, Folklore, Customs, Worship, Festivals, and Superstition, by William Tyler Olcott. ISBN 1-58509-044-1 • 316 pages • 6 x 9 • trade paper • $24.95

Nature Worship: An Account of Phallic Faiths and Practices Ancient and Modern, by the Author of Phallicism with an Introduction by Tedd St. Rain. ISBN 1-58509-049-2 • 112 pages • 6 x 9 • trade paper • illustrated • $12.95

Life and Religion, by Max Muller. ISBN 1-885395-10-8 • 237 pages • 5 1/2 x 8 1/2 • trade paper • $14.95

Jesus: God, Man, or Myth? An Examination of the Evidence, by Herbert Cutner. ISBN 1-58509-072-7 • 304 pages • 6 x 9 • trade paper • $23.95

Pagan and Christian Creeds: Their Origin and Meaning, by Edward Carpenter. ISBN 1-58509-024-7 • 316 pages • 5 1/2 x 8 1/2 • trade paper • $24.95

The Christ Myth: A Study, by Elizabeth Evans. ISBN 1-58509-037-9 • 136 pages • 6 x 9 • trade paper • $13.95

Popery: Foe of the Church and the Republic, by Joseph F. Van Dyke. ISBN 1-58509-058-1 • 336 pages • 6 x 9 • trade paper • illustrated • $25.95

Career of Religious Ideas, by Hudson Tuttle. ISBN 1-58509-066-2 • 172 pages • 5 x 8 • trade paper • $15.95

Buddhist Suttas: Major Scriptural Writings from Early Buddhism, by T.W. Rhys Davids. ISBN 1-58509-079-4 • 376 pages • 6 x 9 • trade paper • $27.95

Early Buddhism, by T. W. Rhys Davids. Includes *Buddhist Ethics: The Way to Salvation?*, by Paul Tice. ISBN 1-58509-076-X • 112 pages • 6 x 9 • trade paper • $12.95

The Fountain-Head of Religion: A Comparative Study of the Principal Religions of the World and a Manifestation of their Common Origin from the Vedas, by Ganga Prasad. ISBN 1-58509-054-9 • 276 pages • 6 x 9 • trade paper • $22.95

India: What Can It Teach Us?, by Max Muller. ISBN 1-58509-064-6 • 284 pages • 5 1/2 x 8 1/2 • trade paper • $22.95

Matrix of Power: How the World has Been Controlled by Powerful People Without Your Knowledge, by Jordan Maxwell. ISBN 1-58509-120-0 • 104 pages • 6 x 9 • trade paper • $12.95

Cyberculture Counterconspiracy: A Steamshovel Web Reader, Volume One, edited by Kenn Thomas. ISBN 1-58509-125-1 • 180 pages • 6 x 9 • trade paper • illustrated • $16.95

Cyberculture Counterconspiracy: A Steamshovel Web Reader, Volume Two, edited by Kenn Thomas. ISBN 1-58509-126-X • 132 pages • 6 x 9 • trade paper • illustrated • $13.95

Oklahoma City Bombing: The Suppressed Truth, by Jon Rappoport. ISBN 1-885395-22-1 • 112 pages • 5 1/2 x 8 1/2 • trade paper • $12.95

The Protocols of the Learned Elders of Zion, by Victor Marsden. ISBN 1-58509-015-8 • 312 pages • 6 x 9 • trade paper • $24.95

Secret Societies and Subversive Movements, by Nesta H. Webster. ISBN 1-58509-092-1 • 432 pages • 6 x 9 • trade paper • $29.95

The Secret Doctrine of the Rosicrucians, by Magus Incognito. ISBN 1-58509-091-3 • 256 pages • 6 x 9 • trade paper • $20.95

The Origin and Evolution of Freemasonry: Connected with the Origin and Evolution of the Human Race, by Albert Churchward. ISBN 1-58509-029-8 • 240 pages • 6 x 9 • trade paper • $18.95

The Lost Key: An Explanation and Application of Masonic Symbols, by Prentiss Tucker. ISBN 1-58509-050-6 • 192 pages • 6 x 9 • trade paper • illustrated • $15.95

The Character, Claims, and Practical Workings of Freemasonry, by Rev. C.G. Finney. ISBN 1-58509-094-8 • 288 pages • 6 x 9 • trade paper • $22.95

The Secret World Government or "The Hidden Hand": The Unrevealed in History, by Maj.-Gen., Count Cherep-Spiridovich. ISBN 1-58509-093-X • 270 pages • 6 x 9 • trade paper • $21.95

The Magus, Book One: A Complete System of Occult Philosophy, by Francis Barrett. ISBN 1-58509-031-X • 200 pages • 6 x 9 • trade paper • illustrated • $16.95

The Magus, Book Two: A Complete System of Occult Philosophy, by Francis Barrett. ISBN 1-58509-032-8 • 220 pages • 6 x 9 • trade paper • illustrated • $17.95

The Magus, Book One and Two: A Complete System of Occult Philosophy, by Francis Barrett. ISBN 1-58509-033-6 • 420 pages • 6 x 9 • trade paper • illustrated • $34.90

The Key of Solomon The King, by S. Liddell MacGregor Mathers. ISBN 1-58509-022-0 • 152 pages • 6 x 9 • trade paper • illustrated • $12.95

Magic and Mystery in Tibet, by Alexandra David-Neel. ISBN 1-58509-097-2 • 352 pages • 6 x 9 • trade paper • $26.95

The Comte de St. Germain, by I. Cooper Oakley. ISBN 1-58509-068-9 • 280 pages • 6 x 9 • trade paper • illustrated • $22.95

Alchemy Rediscovered and Restored, by A. Cockren. ISBN 1-58509-028-X • 156 pages • 5 1/2 x 8 1/2 • trade paper • $13.95

The 6th and 7th Books of Moses, with an Introduction by Paul Tice. ISBN 1-58509-045-X • 188 pages • 6 x 9 • trade paper • illustrated • $16.95

CPSIA information can be obtained at www.ICGtesting.com
Printed in the USA
LVOW10s0020150314

377544LV00013B/193/A

9 781585 091126